*Longman*
*practice kit*

# GCSE
# Biology

*Chris Millican*

LONGMAN

**Series Editors**
Geoff Black and Stuart Wall

**Titles available**
*GCSE*           *A-Level*
Biology          Biology
Business Studies Business Studies
English          Chemistry
Geography        Mathematics
Mathematics      Psychology
Physics          Sociology
Science

Addison Wesley Longman Ltd,
Edinburgh Gate, Harlow,
Essex CM20 2JE, England
*and Associated Companies throughout the World.*

© Addison Wesley Longman 1997

All rights reserved; no part of this publication may be reproduced, stored in a retrieval system, or transmitted in any form or by any means, electronic, mechanical, photocopying, recording or otherwise without either the prior written permission of the Publishers or a licence permitting restricted copying in the United Kingdom issued by the Copyright Licensing Agency Ltd, 90 Tottenham Court Road, London W1P 9HE.

First Published 1997

ISBN 0582-30381-8

British Library Cataloguing-in-Publication Data
A catalogue record for this book is available from the British Library.

Printed in Great Britain by Henry Ling Ltd, at the Dorset Press
Dorchester, Dorset

### Acknowledgements
We are grateful to the following examination boards for permission to reproduce questions from past examination papers:

   Associated Examining Board (AEB)
   EDEXCEL Foundation (ULEAC)
   Midland Examining Group (MEG)
   Northern Ireland Council for Curriculum and Examination (NICCEA)
   Welsh Joint Education Committee (WJEC)

Please note that the answers given are those supplied by the author. In the case of questions supplied by an examination board the answers and hints are still those of the author and the board accepts no responsibility whatsoever for the accuracy or method of working in the answers that are given. Indications of mark schemes have not been approved by the examination board.

I would like to thank Angela Bullard for her help in typing the manuscript and Clive Hurford for his support and encouragement throughout the project.
*Chris Millican*

# Contents

**Part I    Preparing for the examination  1**

**Part II   Topic areas, summaries and questions  7**

*Chapter 1* Life processes and cell activity  *8*

*Chapter 2* Humans as organisms  *12*

*Chapter 3* Green plants as organisms  *23*

*Chapter 4* Variation, inheritance and evolution  *29*

*Chapter 5* Living organisms in their environment  *40*

*Chapter 6* Extension topics  *53*

**Part III  Answers and grading  63**

*Chapter 1* Solutions: Life processes and cell activity  *64*

*Chapter 2* Solutions: Humans as organisms  *65*

*Chapter 3* Solutions: Green plants as organisms  *70*

*Chapter 4* Solutions: Variation, inheritance and evolution  *73*

*Chapter 5* Solutions: Living organisms in their environment  *78*

*Chapter 6* Solutions: Extension topics  *84*

**Part IV   Timed practice paper with answers  89**

**Timed practice paper**  *90*

**Outline answers**  *96*

# How to use this book

This book covers the core topics which are the same for all the examination boards (these are part of the National Curriculum in Science for England and Wales) and some of the more common extension topics (these differ from board to board). In Scotland and Northern Ireland, the syllabus is organised differently, but the topics covered are very similar.

### Part I Preparing for the examination

This includes useful techniques you could use before and during the examination to improve your grade, e.g. a summary of revision strategies, advice on how to tackle the main types of examination questions and a list of key words you will meet in examination questions.

### Part II Topic areas, summaries and questions

This part is divided into six sections; the core areas of the syllabus, common to all examination boards and the sixth covers the main extension topics. In each section you will find the following:
- **Revision tips** Giving specific advice on revising those topic areas.
- **Topic outline** Briefly summarising the key points you are expected to know.
- **Revision activities** To help make your revision active, there are some short revision exercises to help you to self-check your understanding.
- **Practice questions** Questions from recent examination papers.

### Part III Answers and grading

Here you will find answers to the revision activities and practice questions set for each topic area. These are outline answers from the examiners, to indicate what they were looking for in that question.

### Part IV Timed practice paper with answers

Here you will find an examination paper to give you practice in timing yourself under exam-type conditions before the exam. Outline answers and a breakdown of the marks awarded are provided for these questions, so you can check your performance.

*part I*
# Preparing for the examination

# Introduction

Every year I talk to students who say they have worked hard for exams, but who are disappointed by their results. There are several possible reasons for this:

- **They have not worked hard enough** Success demands a lot of time and effort from you; it is quite easy to fool other people into thinking you are working hard but, deep down, you know how much effort you have really made.
- **They have left it too late to start revision** Lots of people put off starting to revise; they feel as though tomorrow will be the ideal day but then they find reasons to delay again. When they finally do start, sometimes with only days to go before the actual examination, they feel rushed and panic. They try to read through all of their work, but have no time to concentrate properly on what they are doing.
- **They are spending time and effort on revision, but are using the wrong techniques** If you are just reading through your notes, it is very easy to let your mind wander. You find yourself staring blankly at the page, or you are actually reading without thinking about the meaning of the words. To be effective, revision must be active, i.e. it must involve you in doing something.
- **They know the facts, but cannot apply them** This happens if you learn something by rote, but do not understand it, e.g. you learn a list of labels for a diagram without learning to recognise the structures, or you learn an explanation 'parrot fashion' but cannot relate it to a particular set of circumstances. Lots of questions ask for recall and understanding, i.e. they may want you to use your theory knowledge in a new context.
- **They do not know what the question wants** Sometimes they cannot recognise which area of the syllabus is being tested, or have no idea what the question is asking. However, if the question is asked in a slightly different way, or if they are prompted (perhaps by an additional question), they are able to gain full marks. You probably recognise this feeling when your teacher goes over a test you have done in class; you can't believe it would have been so easy to get it right!

From this you can see that passing exams is not just a matter of whether you perform well for two hours in the exam itself. There are three steps to success:

1. **Throughout the course** you should be working hard to make sure you **understand** the topics covered. If you have tests in school, look carefully at where you lost marks, and why. If you don't understand a particular section, read about it in a textbook or ask your teacher. Never just leave a section of the syllabus you don't understand.
2. **In the run up to exams** you should be revising the work covered in the course so that you really **know your facts**. First, get your files or books organised and make a list of everything you need to revise. Make a revision plan and stick to it. Use books like this and past exam paper questions to get practice. If your school runs lunchtime or after-school revision lessons, make sure that you go to them!
3. **In the exam** you should be concentrating hard to **show what you know**. This means reading the questions carefully and writing clear, concise answers. Exam technique helps you to know how long an answer should be and to recognise which key words to include for maximum marks. Too many

---

**There are three factors vital for success:**

1. **Understand the work covered**
2. **Learn it thoroughly**
3. **Communicate it clearly in exams**

people lose marks by being vague, or by writing long, waffly answers which suggest that they do not really understand the topic.

There is an element of luck in exams, but a successful student does not depend on being lucky – they work hard to make sure they will do well.

### Planning your revision

- **Start revising early** You may think that you will forget the first things you revise, but this is not the case. Give yourself enough time to cover the whole syllabus at least twice.
- **Organise your books and files** Make sure that your work is complete and that it is in the right order. If you have bits missing you will need to photocopy work from a friend.
- **Make sure that you know what you have to revise** Check with your teacher which syllabus you are studying, and to what level. Some topics will only be tested on higher level papers, so you may not have to learn all of it.
- **Make a revision plan using your topic list** This breaks the work up into manageable chunks and gives you a sense of achievement when you can see you are making progress. You could use the revision planner in this book to help you with this.
- **Make sure you cover all the topics in your revision** Don't try to predict which questions will come up. If you have studied a course for two years, you have probably had 100–150 hours of lessons, but your exams will last only two to three hours; you have to accept that some parts of the syllabus will not be tested, but it is not possible to guess which!
- **Revise actively** This means *do* something, don't just read your notes! You could practise drawing and labelling, make up mnemonics to help you remember facts (like MRS GREN for life processes), write summary notes, write lists of key words on to summary cards, make spider diagrams ... the list is almost endless.
- **Learn definitions and equations properly** You can then recall them straight away. It is far easier to spend a bit of time learning them than to try to make them up in the exam. It is worth practising writing key words as well, to make sure you get the spelling right.
- **Test yourself frequently** Or get someone else to test you. It is easy to test recall with short, verbal answers to a friend or parent. You can find out how well you understand a topic by trying to explain it to someone else – it's even better if they know nothing about it before you start. Think about explaining mitosis, or osmosis, or how the heart beats, and you'll see what I mean. If you get stuck, or you can't explain it simply enough for someone else to follow, go back to your notes, read about it, then try again.

### Using exam questions in revision

Once you have revised a topic, it is very useful to try out some practice questions. This will help you in several ways:
- It shows whether you really understand the topic; if not, go back to your notes.
- You will become familiar with the language used in questions (look at the list of 'command words' on page 5).
- You can check your answers against the outline answers and see how to gain extra marks.
- You can attempt a whole exam paper and time your work, i.e. work under examination conditions.

## Types of examination questions

In Biology GCSE there are eight main types of question:

1. **Short answer** These are very common and often require a one-word or one-phrase answer. You are not expected to answer in a full sentence – there is usually not enough space.
   e.g. What form of energy is necessary for photosynthesis to occur?

   ..................................................................................................................

2. **Longer answer** This is often part of a structured question, and requires a 3–4 line answer. The number of lines available and the number of marks give an indication of the length and detail required in the answer. You are expected to write in sentences, or to produce a well-organised list, but try to make your answer concise.
   e.g. Explain why it is useful for household rubbish to be made into compost. [3]

   ..................................................................................................................

   ..................................................................................................................

   ..................................................................................................................

3. **Extended answer** This is usually an 'essay-type' question worth 8 to 10 marks and you are expected to write between half a page and a whole page. This needs careful thought to decide which facts are relevant, organise them into a coherent answer and to make sure you have answered the question fully.
   e.g. Explain how an increase in the human population can have a harmful effect on the environment. [10]
   You could write about:
   - increased need for food [1], therefore more land needed for farming [1], possible over-use of pesticides and fertilisers to increase yield [1], possible over-fishing [1];
   - increased need for living space, roads, etc. [1], so natural habitats are destroyed [1];
   - increased need for resources, e.g. wood, metal, stone, fuels [1], so natural habitats destroyed by mining, quarrying, etc. [1], deforestation as wood is used for building/fuel [1], or land is cleared for grazing animals [1];
   - increased pollution from homes, industry, cars [1] causes acid rain (sulphur dioxide and nitrogen oxides) [1], increased carbon dioxide linked to the greenhouse effect [1], CFCs (in aerosols, packaging) damage the ozone layer [1], sewage pollutes rivers and the sea [1], farm waste and chemicals leached from fields pollute rivers and the sea [1].

4. **Drawing and labelling diagrams** Make sure you know which diagrams you must be able to draw **and** label, and which you must label only (your teacher will have a list). Practise drawing and labelling them when you are revising.
   Make sure label lines point accurately at the required structures, and always make your diagrams big enough to be clear.

5. **Drawing graphs and bar charts** You may be given a set of axes which are already labelled, sometimes with a scale ready drawn. If not, the following rules apply:
   (a) The independent variable is plotted across the bottom of the graph ($x$-axis), and the dependent variable is plotted along the side of the graph ($y$-axis).
   (b) Use the largest possible scale on the graph paper you are given.
   (c) Make sure that the scales are uniform, i.e. the numbers increase by the same amount across each square.

(d) Label your axes clearly, including units.
(e) Plot points carefully using pencil (you can rub it out if you make mistakes).
(f) Join the points with a straight line or a smooth curve.
(g) If it is a bar chart, use a ruler to draw the bars and label them.

6 **Data analysis** You may be given some data, e.g. in a table, graph, or comprehension passage, and asked questions about it. It is likely that you will not have seen exactly the same material before, but it will relate to part of your syllabus.
   (a) If it is a **table**: look carefully at the column headings and units; you may have to carry out calculations to answer some parts of the question.
   (b) If it is a **graph**: look at the axis labels and units. What are the main trends shown by the graph?
   (c) If it is a **comprehension passage**: read it through carefully at least twice and underline key words.

7 **Simple calculations** These are particularly common in Scottish Examination Board questions, although most exam boards set some calculations. You should be able to:
   (a) carry out simple addition, subtraction, multiplication and division
   (b) calculate ratios
   (c) calculate percentages
   (d) calculate averages.
   Remember, you must always show your working, and include units in your answer.

8 **Describing experiments** You should be able to draw labelled diagrams of apparatus and explain the key features of common experiments.
   e.g. Photosynthesis experiments (with pondweed); food tests (for sugar, starch).

## COMMAND WORDS USED IN EXAMINATIONS

**Describe** Give an outline of the process or structure. Include key points.

**Explain** Give biological reasons to account for what is happening.

**State** Give a simple description/definition.

**Suggest** Give possible reasons/explanations. You are not expected to recall an answer here, but should give reasonable suggestions.

**Compare** Look for similarities and differences. Make sure your answer relates to both parts of the question.

**Define** Give a concise definition. Do not use the 'question word' in your answer.

**Summarise** Write the key points.

**Discuss** Give the points for and against. This word is normally used in longer or extended prose answers.

**Give an account of** Describe the process which is occurring or methods used in the experiment. Make sure that your answer is written in a logical sequence.

### Assessment objectives in biology

The examination will test your ability to:
(a) carry out experimental and investigative work (25%)
(b) recall, understand, use and apply biological knowledge (60%)

(c) communicate biological observations, ideas and arguments (using appropriate vocabulary), and evaluate biological information (15%)

**Important points**
- experimental and investigative work is assessed by coursework;
- the written examinations count for 75 per cent of your total mark;
- 40 per cent is for understanding, use and application of knowledge, 20 per cent is for recall of knowledge.

*Scheme of assessment*

From 1998, examination boards will set papers at two different tiers, leading to different grades. The names for the tiers vary between boards, but the basic pattern is like this:

> Foundation/Basic Tier – Grades C–G
> Higher Tier – Grades A*–D

Most exam boards set two written papers, lasting a total of 2–3 hours, in addition to coursework.

## During the exam

- Make sure you have the right equipment with you, i.e. pencils, pens, rubber, ruler, calculator.
- Read the instructions on the front of the exam paper.
- Look at the number of questions to be answered and plan your time roughly.

**When you are about to answer a question:**
- Read the question carefully and underline key words.
- Decide which part of the syllabus is being tested. Remember, a question may require information from different parts of the syllabus:
  e.g. a question on exercise may include information on muscles, heart rate, respiration and lactic acid;
  a question on blood may include information on transport, immunity and genetics (blood groups or haemophilia).
- Look at the number of lines and number of marks available to decide the amount of detail needed.
- Keep an eye on the time, and check your progress through the paper after 30 minutes and 1 hour.
- If you get stuck, mark the question (in pencil), leave it and get on with other questions. Return to it if you have time.
- If you finish early, go back and check that you have completed all the questions, and read over your answers.

*part II*
# Topic areas, summaries and questions

# 1 Life processes and cell activity

## REVISION TIPS

This topic contains some very basic information, e.g. locations and functions of organs in humans and flowering plants, so make sure you can label the obvious diagrams. You should be able to relate structure to function in different types of cells and you must recognise diagrams of the main cell types.

It is vital to learn definitions for diffusion, osmosis and active transport. Questions on this topic are often tested with data questions, so you must be able to apply your knowledge.

Make sure that you can spell mitosis and meiosis and that you know the key features of each. You may have to put a set of diagrams or a list of steps into the correct order, or to compare the two processes.

## TOPIC OUTLINE

- There are **7** important life processes shown by all living things. Remember MRS GREN!
- Multicellular organisms often show division of labour. **Cells** are grouped into **organs**, and **organs** are grouped into **systems** so that the organism can function efficiently.
- You must be able to label and state the functions of important organs in humans and flowering plants.
- The basic unit of all living things is the **cell**.
- All cells consist of a **cell membrane**, **cytoplasm** and **nucleus** (containing **genes**). **Plant cells** also have a **cell wall** and **sap vacuole**, and some have **chloroplasts** (for photosynthesis).
- Cells are specialised so that they can carry out particular functions efficiently, e.g. red blood cells have haemoglobin to carry oxygen; root hair cells have a long root hair to increase the surface area for absorption.
- Substances can move in and out of cells in **3** ways: diffusion, osmosis and active transport.
- **Diffusion** is the movement of a substance from an area where there is a high concentration to an area where there is a lower concentration, until it is evenly distributed.
- **Osmosis** is the movement of water through a semi-permeable membrane from an area where there is a high concentration of water molecules to an area where there is a lower concentration of water molecules.
- **Active transport** is the movement of a substance against a concentration gradient. It can only occur in living cells, because it requires energy.
- There are two types of cell division: **mitosis** and **meiosis**.
- **Mitosis** occurs in body cells and it makes **2** daughter cells which are identical to the parent cell.
- **Meiosis** occurs during gamete formation and it makes **4** daughter cells, each of which has half as many chromosomes as the parent cell.
- **Genes** are units of inherited information (they are part of chromosomes inside the nucleus).

# life processes and cell activity

## REVISION ACTIVITY

**1** Complete this table about the parts of a cell.

| Part | Function |
|---|---|
|  | controls what enters and leaves the cells |
|  | contains chlorophyll |
|  | contains genes |
|  | chemical reactions, e.g. protein synthesis, occur here |

**2** Identify these cells, and state two ways that each is adapted for its function:

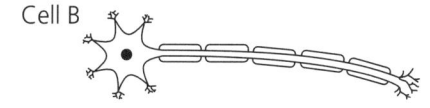

Cell A          Cell B

**3** State three differences between plant and animal cells.

**4** Fill in the gaps to complete this definition of osmosis.
Osmosis is the movement of _____ from an area of _____ concentration of water to an area of _____ concentration of water, through a _____.

**5** If you left this apparatus for one hour, what change would you see? Explain why.

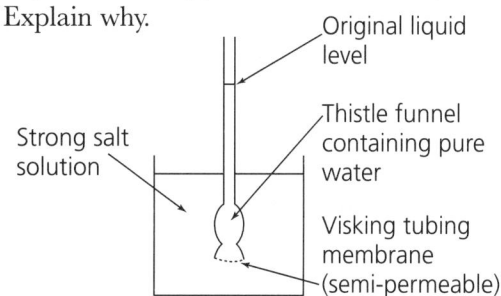

- Original liquid level
- Thistle funnel containing pure water
- Strong salt solution
- Visking tubing membrane (semi-permeable)

**6** Pieces of potato were carefully cut and their length, diameter and mass were measured. They were placed in solution X for 2 hours, then re-measured. Look at the results table and use it to answer the questions.

|  | Original | Final | Difference |
|---|---|---|---|
| Length (mm) | 40 | 43 |  |
| Diameter (mm) | 10 | 11 |  |
| Mass (g) | 2 | 2.4 |  |

Why did the potato pieces change? Suggest what solution X might be.

**7** Read these statements about mitosis, then put them into the correct order.
**A** chromatids move to the poles of the cell
**B** chromosomes become shorter and thicker
**C** each chromosome makes a copy of itself so it is made up of 2 chromatids
**D** chromosomes line up across the middle (equator) of the cell
**E** the cell divides into 2 parts
Correct order: _____

**8.** Give three differences between mitosis and meiosis.

## EXAMINATION QUESTIONS

### Question 1
(a) The diagram below shows a side view of the human body and some organs. The key lists the organs shown in the diagram.
Write the correct letter for each organ on the diagram in the boxes provided.

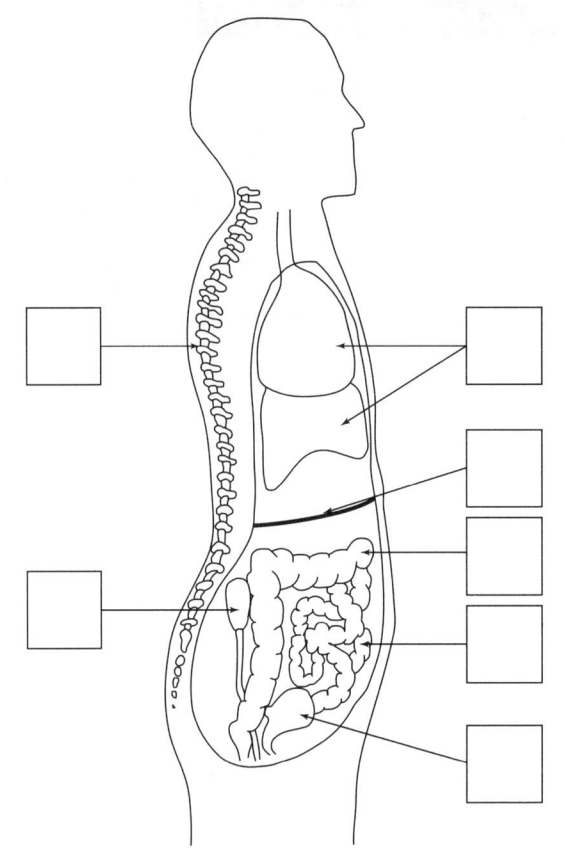

| Organ | Letter |
|---|---|
| Bladder | A |
| Brain | B |
| Diaphragm | C |
| Kidney | D |
| Large intestine | E |
| Lungs | F |
| Small intestine | G |
| Vertebral column | H |

[7]

(b) On the diagram, write an X to show the position of the heart. [1]

**Total 8 marks**
[ULEAC]

### Question 2
Table 1 below lists some human organs. Table 2 lists some of the functions of these organs.

**Table 1**

| Human organ | Letter |
|---|---|
| Brain | A |
| Lung | B |
| Diaphragm | C |
| Liver | D |
| Small intestine | E |
| Kidney | F |
| Bladder | G |
| Penis | H |

**Table 2**

| Function of organ | Letter |
|---|---|
| Makes urea, a waste product | D |
| Stores urine | |
| Moves downwards to help us breathe in | |
| Filters the blood to remove toxic substances such as urea | |
| Absorbs useful substances from the food we eat | |
| Receives impulses which allow us to see and hear | |
| Takes in oxygen and gives out carbon dioxide | |
| Passes urine and sperms out of the body | |
| Controls the movement of our legs when we walk | |

Complete Table 2 by writing ONE letter in each empty box to link the function with the correct organ. You may use each letter once, more than once or not at all. The first one has been done for you. [8]

[ULEAC]

### Question 3
A pupil investigated osmosis using uncooked potato chips and Visking tubing bags. Two different varieties of potato, *Cara* and *Rocket*, were each tested separately, and the chips were all the same size and shape.

The Visking tubing bags were of equal size and contained a ten per cent (10%) sugar solution. They were carefully sealed to avoid leaks.

The chips and the Visking tubing were then tied to the ends of a balance and immersed into concentrated sugar solution and water.

Three sets of apparatus were used, one for potato *Cara*, one for potato *Rocket* and one for the Visking tubing bags.

The diagrams below show each set of apparatus before and after the experiment.

| Apparatus at start of the experiment | Apparatus after one hour of the experiment | Angle measured in degrees (average from 5 repeated experiments) |
|---|---|---|
| Concentrated sugar solution / Distilled water / Potato chip (*Cara*) / Potato chip (*Cara*) | Protractor Angle measured | 15.5 |
| Concentrated sugar solution / Distilled water / Potato chip (*Rocket*) / Potato chip (*Rocket*) | Protractor Angle measured | 26.0 |
| Concentrated sugar solution / Distilled water / Visking tubing bag with 10% sugar solution / Visking tubing bag with 10% sugar solution | Protractor Angle measured | 15.5 |

(a) The balance beam became higher on the left hand side but lower on the right hand side at the end of each experiment. Explain why this happened. [4]

(b) What is the approximate concentration of the sap inside the potato cells of the variety *Cara*? Give a reason. [2]

**Total 6 marks**

[ULEAC]

# Humans as organisms

## REVISION TIPS

This is a huge part of the syllabus. It includes information about body systems, e.g. circulatory, digestive, respiratory and excretory systems; about co-ordination (nerves and hormones); about homeostasis (skin and temperature control, water balance) and about health (defence against infection, immunity and drugs).

You will have to spend a lot of time on revising this section, so that you are familiar with all the information.

Make sure you can label key diagrams, e.g. heart, circulatory system, respiratory system, reflex arc, eye, nephron.

Extended prose questions may be set on some parts of this topic, e.g. comparing kidney dialysis with kidney transplants;
use of hormones in the control of human fertility;
use and misuse of drugs.

## TOPIC OUTLINE

### Nutrition/digestion

- Humans need a balanced diet to remain healthy.
- There are **seven food groups** in a balanced diet (carbohydrate, protein, lipid, vitamins, minerals, fibre and water).
- **Enzymes** are chemicals produced by the body to speed up digestion.
- Each enzyme has a specific function (e.g. proteases digest protein) and works best at its optimum temperature and pH.
- **Digestion** involves breakdown of large insoluble food molecules to form small, soluble food molecules.
- Digested food is absorbed by the blood, then used by body cells.

### Circulation

- **Blood** is the transport fluid of the body and it is also important in defence against disease.
- The heart **beats** (contracts) to move blood around the body.
- **Veins** carry blood towards the heart and **arteries** carry blood away from the heart. **Capillaries** carry blood through body organs.
- Substances are exchanged between blood and body cells in the capillaries.
- Humans have a **double circulation** (blood travels through the heart twice on each complete circuit of the body).

### Gas exchange and respiration

- **Gas exchange** occurs in the **alveoli**, which are very well adapted (large surface area, thin permeable wall, moist, good blood supply).
- The **ribs** and **diaphragm** move to force air in and out of the lungs.

- **Respiration** is an important chemical reaction occurring in all cells to make energy.
- When oxygen is available, aerobic respiration occurs.

    oxygen + glucose → energy + carbon dioxide + water

- During exercise, when insufficient oxygen is available, anaerobic respiration can occur in muscle cells.

    glucose → energy + lactic acid.

    This is less efficient than aerobic respiration, and produces less energy.

## Movement

- When muscles **contract**, they pull bones of the skeleton closer together.
- Muscles always work in **antagonistic pairs**, e.g. biceps and triceps. An antagonistic pair of muscles have opposite effects to each other.

## Reproduction

- Human reproduction involves the joining of male and female **gametes** (sperm and ovum). This happens inside the **fallopian tube**, after sexual intercourse, and a **zygote** is formed.
- The zygote divides by mitosis to form an **embryo**, and the embryo implants in the **uterus** lining. It will grow and develop in the uterus throughout pregnancy (9 months).
- The **placenta** is a very important organ in pregnancy. It acts as a life support system for the foetus, delivering food and oxygen and removing waste products.
- After 9 months of pregnancy, the foetus is fully developed and is ready to be born. The muscles of the uterus wall contract and the cervix widens so the baby is forced out through the vagina. The umbilical cord is then clamped and cut, and the placenta and remains of the umbilical cord (afterbirth) are pushed out of the uterus.

## Co ordination systems

- Complex, multi-cellular organisms like humans need co-ordination systems to regulate body activities. Humans have **two** co-ordination systems: the **nervous system** and the **endocrine system**.
- The **nervous system** is made up of the brain, spinal cord, nerves and sense organs.
- The **brain** is a complex organ controlling the majority of body functions.
- **Nerve cells** are adapted to carry nerve impulses around the body. They have a long **nerve fibre** (axon) and a **myelin sheath** to speed up transmission of impulses. The junction between nerves is called a **synapse**, and neurotransmitter chemicals are released to diffuse across the small gap between nerve cells.
- A **reflex** is an immediate, unlearned response to a stimulus. Reflexes are very rapid responses and often protect the individual from danger, or increase its chances of survival.
- A **reflex arc** involves only three neurones and does not involve the brain in making decisions.
- **Sense organs** contain receptor cells to detect stimuli.
- The **retina** of the **eye** contains light-sensitive rod and cone cells which send nerve impulses through the optic nerve to the brain.

- The size of the **pupil** changes depending on the amount of light entering the eye, when muscles in the **iris** contract and relax.
- The **ciliary muscle** can contract or relax to change the shape of the **lens**. This is necessary so that the lens can focus light rays effectively on the retina (it is called accommodation).
- The **endocrine system** is made up of **glands** which release **hormones** directly into the blood.
- **Hormones** are chemicals which have an effect on target organs in the body.
- **Insulin** and **glucagon** (made by the pancreas) control **blood sugar levels** in the body. Diabetics do not make enough insulin and may need to be given injections.
- **Sex hormones** (oestrogen, progesterone and testosterone) control puberty, gamete production and the menstrual cycle.
- Female sex hormones can be given artificially to increase or decrease fertility.
- **Adrenaline** is produced by the adrenal glands at times of stress or danger (fight or flight hormone). It has an effect on many target organs of the body.

### Homeostasis

- **Homeostasis** means keeping conditions inside the body constant at an optimum level. This is necessary so that the body can work efficiently.
- Regulation of body temperature, blood sugar levels, water balance and removal of waste products are all examples of homeostasis.
- **Body temperature** is regulated by the **skin**. The main mechanisms involved are **vasodilation** (widening of capillaries) if temperature increases, and **vasoconstriction** if temperature decreases. Sweating, shivering and erection of skin hairs also occur to regulate temperature.
- The **kidney** is responsible for excretion of **urea**, a poisonous substance made in the liver, and for **water balance**.
- The **nephrons** (kidney tubules) are the site of ultrafiltration and reabsorption of useful materials.
- Waste products (water, urea, salts) pass through the **ureters** to the **bladder** and are removed in **urine**.
- The amount of urine produced depends on the levels of excess water in the body.
- **ADH** is a hormone which regulates the amount of water in urine.
- If the kidneys fail, harmful waste products and water accumulate in the body and cause illness. This can be avoided by kidney dialysis or a kidney transplant.
- The **placenta** maintains constant conditions for the foetus during pregnancy.

### Being healthy

- The body has several structures to prevent the entry of pathogens,
  e.g. tough, waterproof skin;
  cilia and mucus to trap pathogens in the respiratory tract;
  acid in the stomach to kill pathogens.
- **White blood cells** attack pathogens which enter the body.
- **Phagocytes** engulf and destroy pathogens.
- **Lymphocytes** make antibodies to destroy pathogens – this is immunity.
- **Vaccination** (deliberate exposure to harmless antigens) makes a person immune to a particular pathogen.
- Drugs are chemicals which change the way the body works. All drugs carry a risk for the person who uses them.

## humans as organisms

### REVISION ACTIVITY

1  Complete this table about the main food groups.

| Food group | Foods containing it | Functions in the body |
|---|---|---|
| Carbohydrate | | |
| | butter, cheese, red meat, fried foods | |
| | | growth and repair, making enzymes |
| | | keeps the digestive system healthy, prevents constipation |
| | meat, milk, green vegetables | |
| | | prevent scurvy and rickets. Needed for healthy skin and bones |

2  Label this diagram of the digestive system.

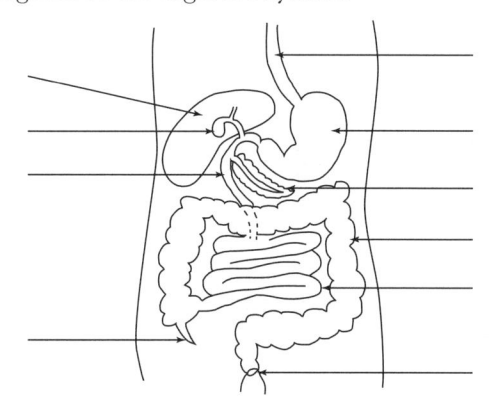

3  What are enzymes?
Look at these graphs showing enzyme activity in different conditions.

A  Enzyme activity

B  Enzyme activity

Which condition is being investigated in Graph A? ___ Graph B? ___

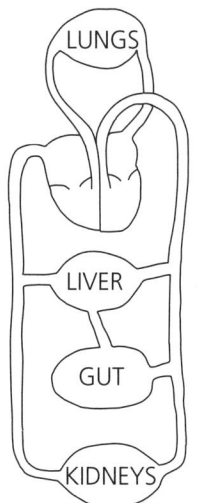

4  Label the following structures:

A  Left ventricle
B  Aorta
C  Vena cava
D  Renal vein
E  Hepatic portal vein
F  Pulmonary artery

What is unusual about the pulmonary artery?

5  Underline the correct alternative to complete the sentences.
When a person breathes in, the diaphragm (contracts/relaxes) so it becomes more (flat/dome-shaped). The external intercostal muscles

(contract/relax) so the rib cage moves (down and in/up and out). The volume of the thorax (decreases/increases) so the pressure in the thorax (decreases/increases) and air moves (in/out).

6  Complete the diagram of the alveolus by:
   (a) drawing in the capillary wall and blood cells
   (b) adding labelled arrows to show how oxygen and carbon dioxide move
   How is the alveolus adapted for gas exchange?

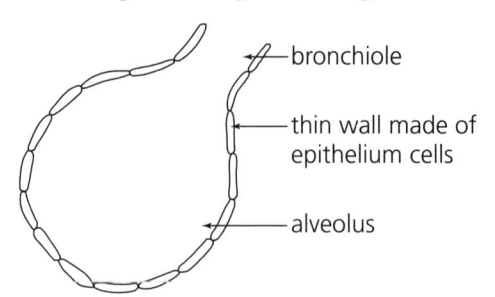

7  Write the respiration equation.

   _____ + _____ → _____ + _____ + _____

8  Complete the table to show the effect of exercise on the body.

| Factor | Increases/Decreases/ Stays the same | Reason |
|---|---|---|
| Heart rate | | |
| Breathing rate | | |
| Lactic acid | | |
| Glycogen in liver/muscle | | |
| Body temperature | | |

9  Put these statements about a reflex arc in the correct order.
   A  impulse passes through motor neurone
   B  receptor detects stimulus
   C  impulse passes through relay neurone
   D  effector responds, e.g. muscle contracts
   E  impulse passes through sensory neurone
   Correct order: _____

10 Fill in the spaces to complete these sentences about the eye.
   Light enters the eye through a hole called the ___. This changes in diameter when muscles in the ___ contract, so the amount of light entering the eye varies. The light is focused on to the ___ by the ___. This changes shape when the ___ muscle contracts or relaxes. To look at a distant object, the lens must be ___ and ___, so the ciliary muscle is ___. The retina contains two types of light-sensitive cells, called ___ and ___; the ___ are most common near to the ___ spot, and they are capable of detecting ___.

11 Answer these questions about the menstrual cycle.
   (a) How long is it?
   (b) On which days:
       (i)  does ovulation occur?
       (ii) does menstruation occur?
       (iii) is fertilisation most likely?
   (c) Which two hormones control the cycle?
   (d) Which is made by the yellow body and placenta?

12 On the diagram of the skin on page 17, label:
   A  the sweat gland         C  the hair erector muscle
   B  a capillary              D  fat cells

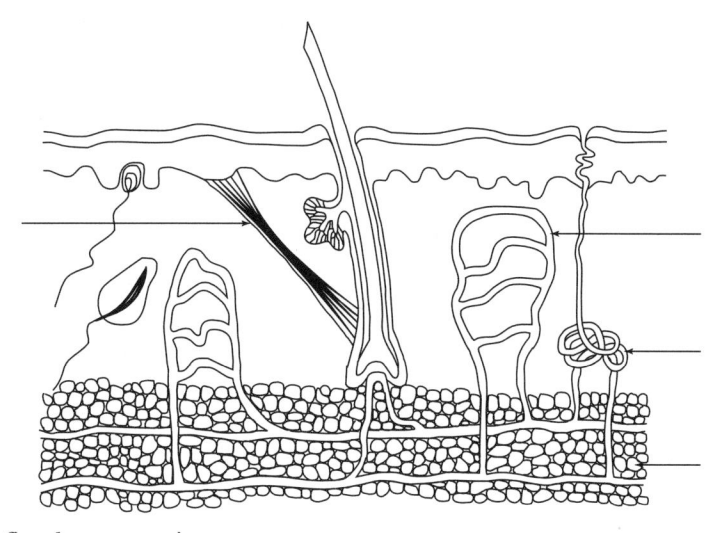

**13** Define homeostasis.

Complete this table about hormones:

| Hormone | Gland making it | Target organ | Effect |
|---|---|---|---|
| Insulin | | | |
| ADH | | | |
| Adrenaline | | | |

## EXAMINATION QUESTIONS

### Question 1

The diagram represents part of the digestive system of a human.

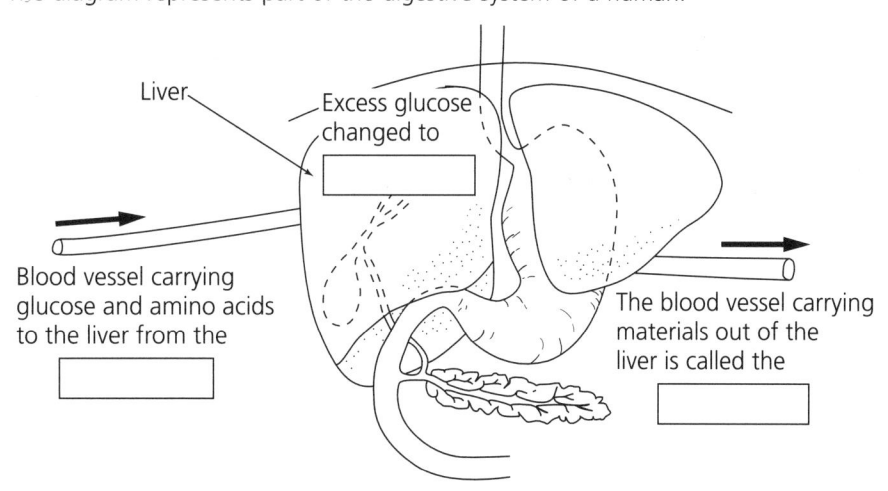

(a) (i) On the diagram, label with an X the connection of the pancreas to the alimentary canal. [1]
(ii) Complete the diagram by writing in the boxes the correct words selected from the list below. [3]

*Hepatic artery   hepatic vein   glycogen   sugar   urine   urea   ileum   pancreas*

(b) Complete the table below to show the chemical elements present in the foods listed.

| Class of food | Chemical elements present |
|---|---|
| Carbohydrate | |
| Protein | |
| Fat | |

[3]

(c) Underline the correct answer below. Digestive enzymes are essential because they
   (i) are protein
   (ii) are unchanged after a reaction
   (iii) can help break down large molecules
   (iv) are denatured by high temperatures [1]
(d) If the normal body temperature is 37°C, which of the following graphs is correct for the human body? [1]

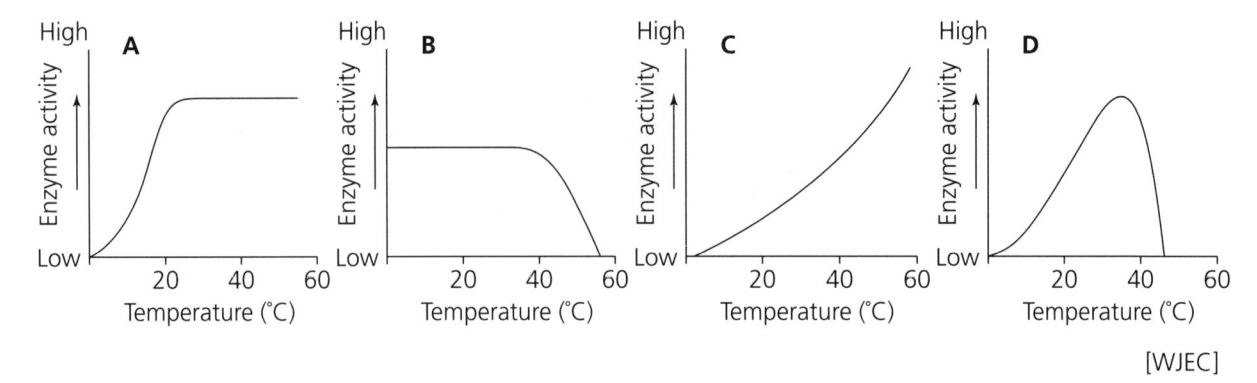

[WJEC]

## Question 2
Bronchitis is an infection of the bronchial tubes which lead to the lungs.

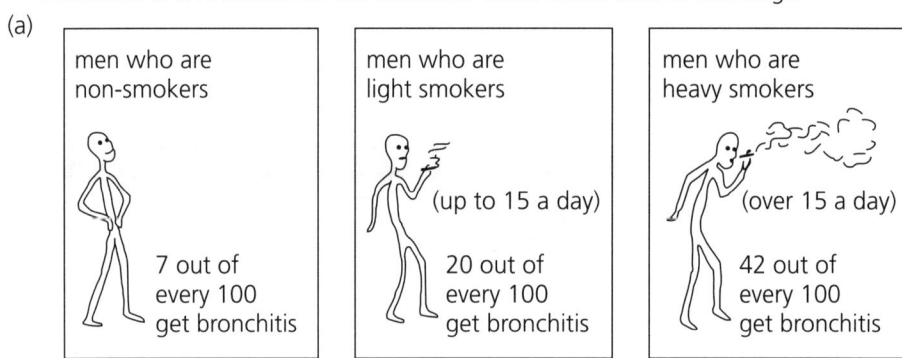

(a) 
- men who are non-smokers: 7 out of every 100 get bronchitis
- men who are light smokers (up to 15 a day): 20 out of every 100 get bronchitis
- men who are heavy smokers (over 15 a day): 42 out of every 100 get bronchitis

What general pattern is shown by this information? [1]

(b) The diagrams show the effects of cigarette smoke on small hairs called cilia in the bronchial tubes.

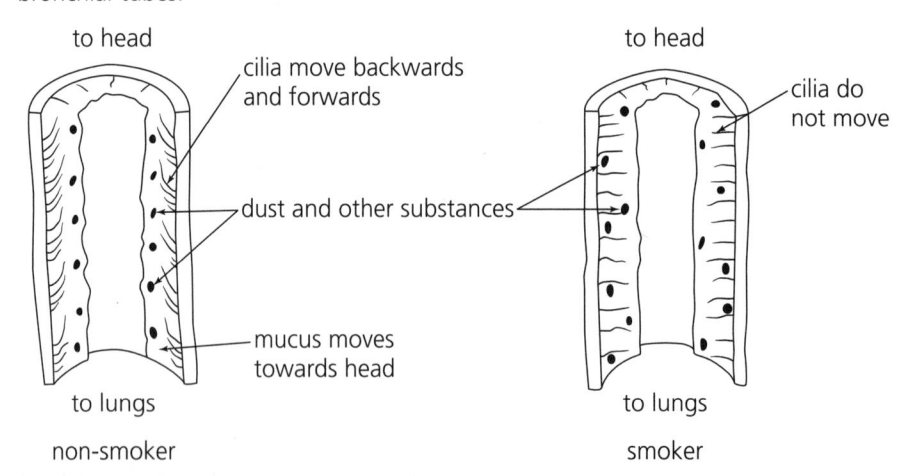

   (i) What effect does cigarette smoke have on the movement of mucus? [1]
   (ii) Suggest why smokers tend to cough more than non-smokers. [2]
   (iii) Smokers are sometimes short of breath. Suggest how smoking affects the lungs to cause this. [2]
(c) The graph shows death rates due to bronchitis in men and women.

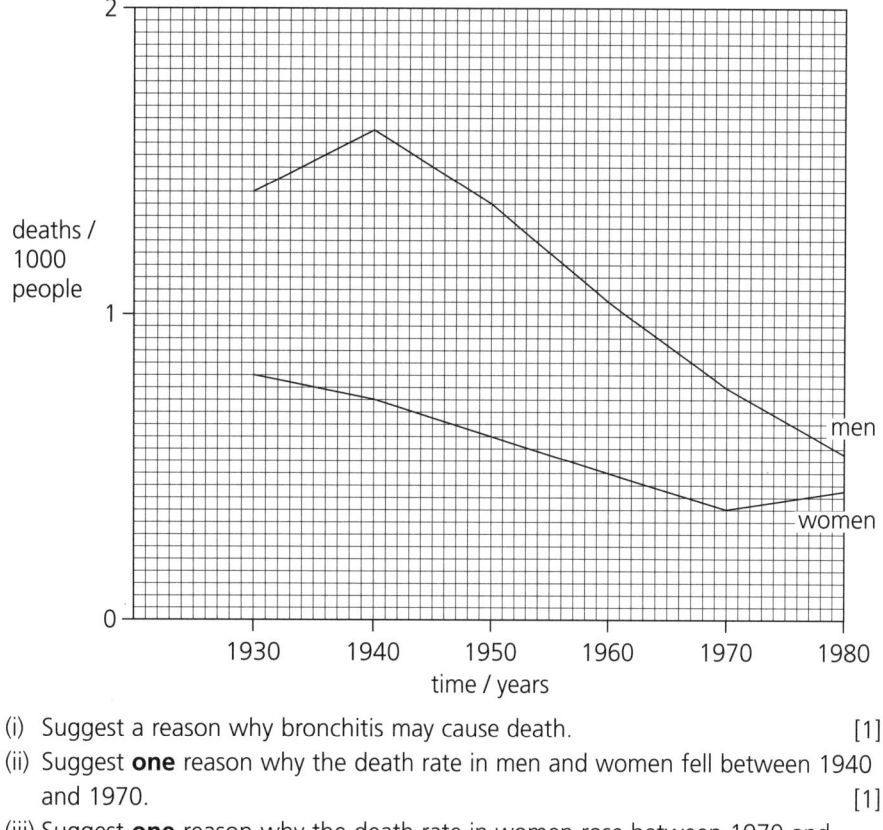

(i) Suggest a reason why bronchitis may cause death. [1]
(ii) Suggest **one** reason why the death rate in men and women fell between 1940 and 1970. [1]
(iii) Suggest **one** reason why the death rate in women rose between 1970 and 1980. [1]
(d) We take air into our bodies so that we can respire.
 (i) Where does respiration take place? [1]
 (ii) Why do we respire? [1]
[MEG]

## Question 3
Fig. 1 shows the structure of the human eye.

*Fig. 1*

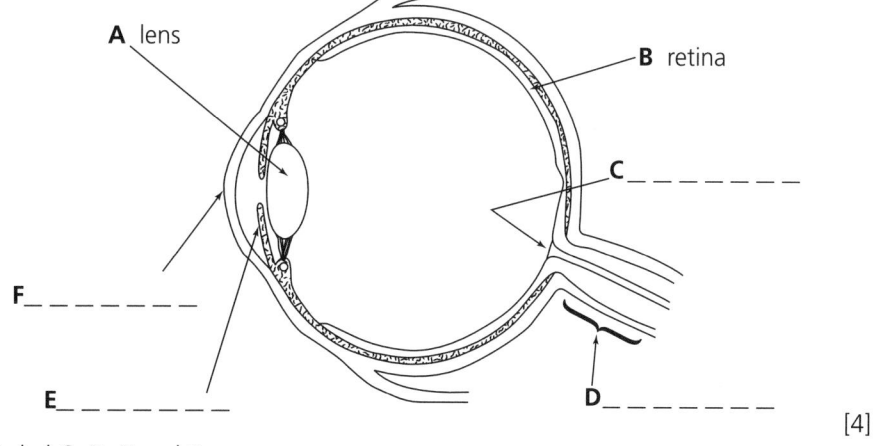

(a) Label **C**, **D**, **E** and **F**. [4]
(b) Describe the functions of **A** (lens) and **B** (retina) [2]
(c) Table 1 below shows the results of an experiment to work out the effect of alcohol on reaction times. A 100 cm rule was placed just above the finger and thumb of an adult volunteer. When released the ruler fell vertically between the finger and thumb. The volunteer was asked to trap the rule as soon as possible after its release. The distance travelled by the rule before it was trapped was recorded. Just before each test, except for the last one, the volunteer drank one unit of whisky. The maximum amount of alcohol the body can get rid of is one unit per hour.

**Table 1**

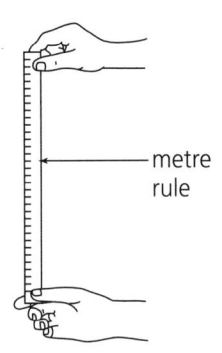

| Time from start/minutes | Distance fallen by rule/cm |
|---|---|
| 0 | 8 |
| 20 | 11 |
| 40 | 15 |
| 60 | 23 |
| 80 | 30 |
| 100 | 42 |
| 120 | 72 |

(i) How many whiskies had the volunteer drunk in the experiment by the time the last test was carried out? [1]

(ii) Look at the distance the ruler fell in the first and last tests. How many times further did the ruler fall in the last test? Show your working. [2]

[MEG]

### Question 4

A woman's regular menstrual cycle lasts 28 days. The diagrams and graph below show changes occurring over 36 days. There are changes in her uterus, ovaries and blood.

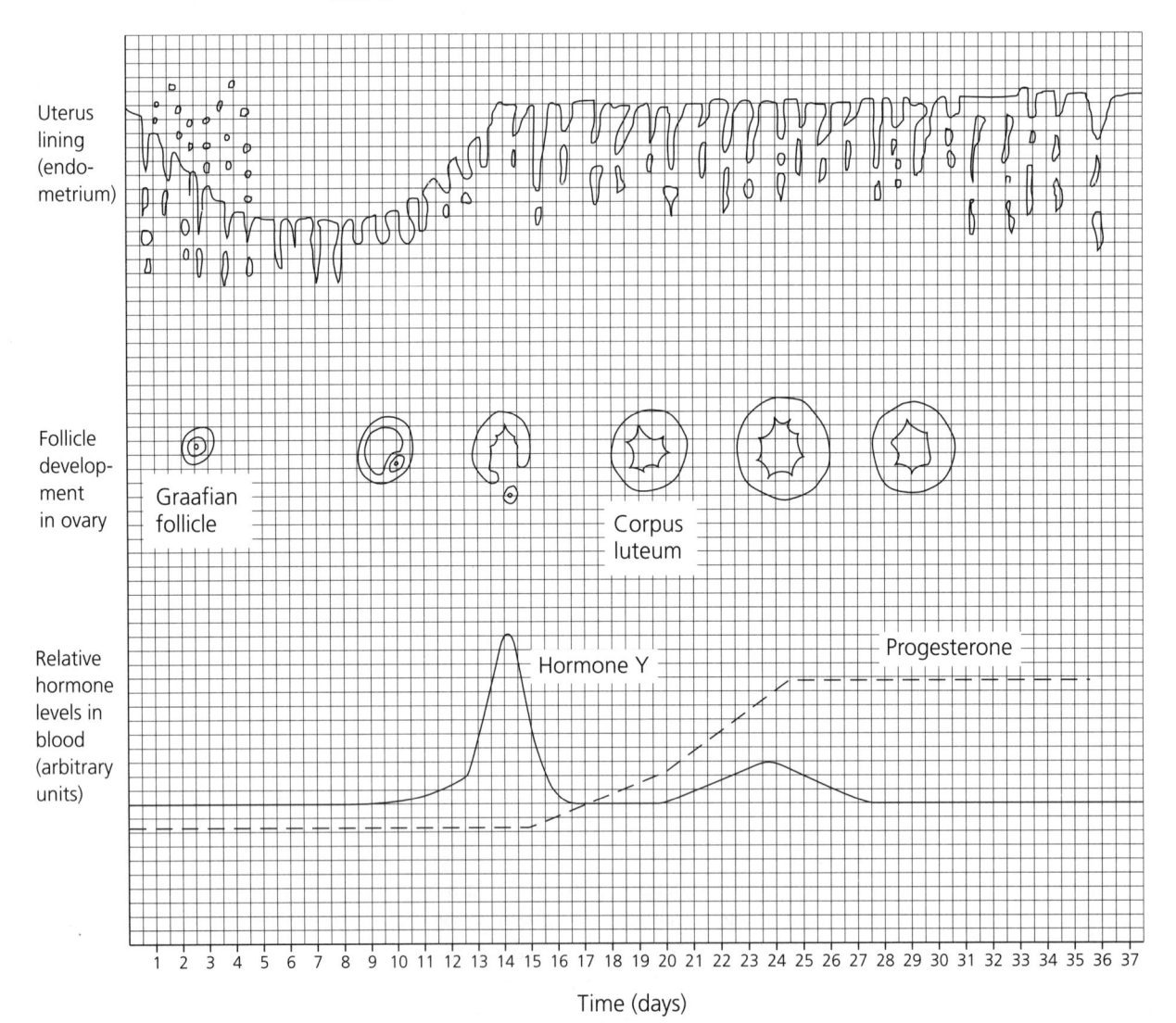

(a) Use the information above and your own knowledge to answer the following questions.
   (i) Suggest TWO effects which result from an increase of hormone Y. [2]
   (ii) Name hormone Y. [1]

(b) (i) Name the process which took place from day 1 to day 5. [1]
   (ii) Which change in hormone level causes this process to begin on day 1? [2]
(c) After 28 days the level of progesterone in the woman's blood remained high.
   (i) State ONE effect of a high level of progesterone. [1]
   (ii) Give TWO reasons why her level of progesterone remained high. [2]
(d) The flow diagram below shows a mechanism which regulates progesterone secretion and ovulation.

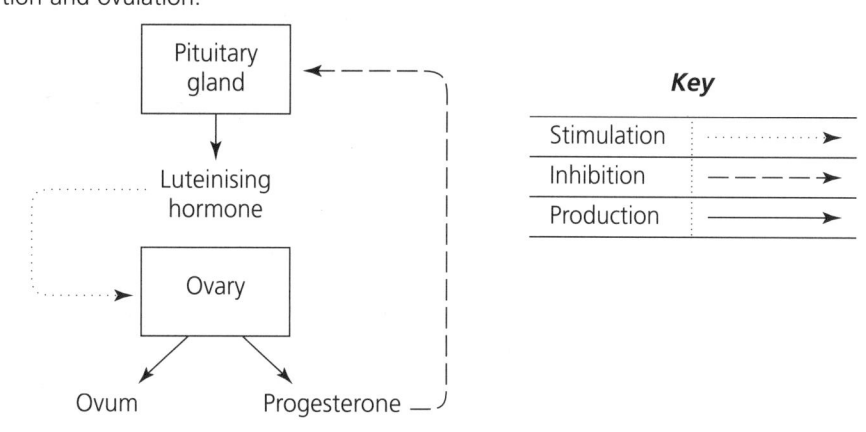

*Key*

Stimulation ·······►
Inhibition – – – →
Production ──────►

Use the information in the flow diagram to help you answer the following questions.
   (i) What effect would low progesterone have on ovulation? Give a reason for your answer. [2]
   (ii) What type of regulatory mechanism is shown by the flow diagram? [2]

**Total 13 marks**
[ULEAC]

### Question 5
(a) What is excretion? [2]
(b) The diagram below shows a section through a human kidney and the vessels connected to it.

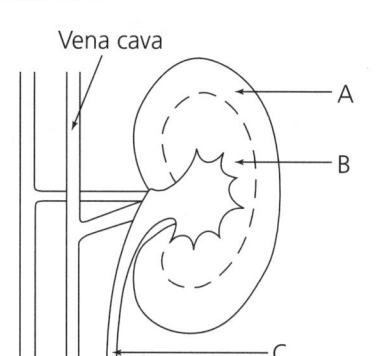

   (i) Name the parts labelled A, B and C. [3]
   (ii) Name the liquid carried in C. [1]
   (iii) To which organ does C lead? [1]
   (iv) On the diagram, use the letter D to label the vessel carrying blood into the kidney. [1]

(c) The table below shows the percentage composition of blood and urine.

| Chemical | Percentage composition | |
|---|---|---|
| | *Blood* | *Urine* |
| Water | 92.00 | 95.00 |
| Protein | 7.00 | 0.00 |
| Glucose | 0.10 | 0.00 |
| Salt | 0.37 | 0.60 |
| Urea | 0.03 | 2.00 |
| Others | 0.50 | 2.40 |

   (i) Name ONE substance which is present in the blood but not in the urine. Explain your answer. [2]
   (ii) Explain why urea is more concentrated in the urine than in the blood. [2]

[NICCEA]

## Question 6
The diagram shows a foetus and part of its placenta.

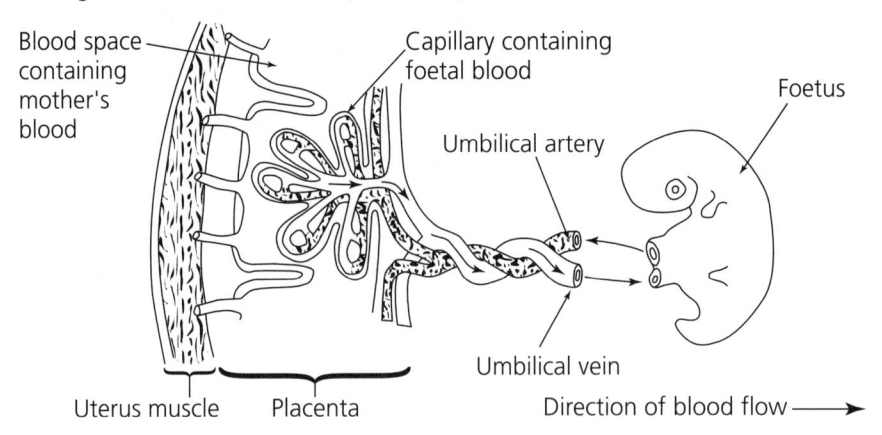

Use the information in the diagram to answer the following questions.
(a) Which blood vessel contains the greatest concentration of oxygen? [1]
(b) Name **two** chemicals which are in greater concentration in the umbilical artery than in the umbilical vein. [2]
(c) How does the foetus use the glucose it receives from the mother? [1]
(d) The diagram shows folding in the placenta. Suggest why this is advantageous to the foetus. [2]

[NICCEA]

## Question 7
(a) The table below records the number of children with measles, in the Eastern Health and Social Services Board (EHSSB), from 1974 to 1981.

| Year | 1974 | 1975 | 1976 | 1977 | 1978 | 1979 | 1980 | 1981 |
|---|---|---|---|---|---|---|---|---|
| Number of children with measles | 300 | 4800 | 200 | 3700 | 200 | 2400 | 700 | 1700 |

(i) Use the information in the table to complete the graph. [4]

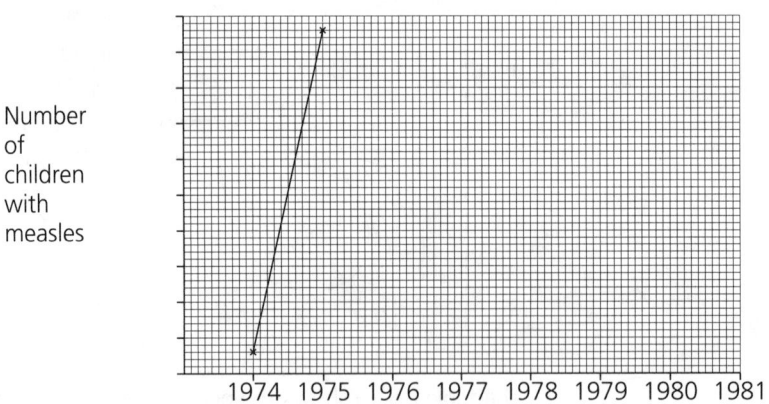

(ii) In which year was the greatest number of children with measles recorded? [1]
(iii) Describe the changes in the numbers of children with measles from 1975 to 1979. [2]

(b) Most young children are immunised (vaccinated) against measles using a weakened form of the measles antigen.
(i) What type of immunity will an immunised child have against measles? [1]
(ii) Explain how immunisation prevents a child developing the disease.
Use the following phrases in your explanation:
   level of antibodies in blood        immunity of child
   measles antibodies                  measles antigen        [4]
(iii) Explain why a one-month-old breast-fed baby would be unlikely to develop measles. [2]

[NICCEA]

# 3 Green plants as organisms

## REVISION TIPS

This topic contains information about leaf structure, photosynthesis, transport in plants and plant hormones. You must know the photosynthesis equation and how the structure of the leaf makes it well adapted for photosynthesis. Make sure you are familiar with all the common photosynthesis experiments and that you understand how limiting factors determine the rate. Learn the definitions of diffusion, osmosis and active transport (see page 8) and know how these are involved in plant transport. Data questions on transpiration are common and require an understanding of the factors which affect transpiration rate. You should know the main functions of hormones in plants and how these can be used by farmers and gardeners to increase crop yield.

## TOPIC OUTLINE

### Photosynthesis

- Leaves are thin and flat and have specialised cells to enable them to carry out **photosynthesis** and **transpiration**.
- Photosynthesis is the way plants make sugar in the light.

$$\text{carbon dioxide} + \text{water} \xrightarrow{\text{light}} \text{glucose} + \text{oxygen}$$

- If any raw materials are in short supply, or if conditions are wrong, the rate of photosynthesis will be slowed down – the factor determining the rate is called the **limiting factor**.
- Sugar made in photosynthesis can be used in respiration, stored as starch or converted to other materials, e.g. protein, chlorophyll.
- Plants carry out **respiration** at all times to make energy.
- When the rate of photosynthesis equals the rate of respiration, we call this the **compensation point**. It occurs in dim light.

### Movement of substances

- Plants need a variety of **minerals**, including nitrate and magnesium, to develop properly. They get these minerals from the soil.
- Plants absorb water by **osmosis** through their root hairs. Water travels upwards through **xylem vessels** due to **transpiration**.
- **Transpiration** is the loss of water through **stomata** on the underside of leaves by evaporation. **Transpiration rate** depends on external factors, e.g. temperature, humidity, amount of light, amount of wind.
- Transpiration rate can be measured using a **potometer**.
- Plants absorb minerals by **diffusion** and **active transport** through their root hairs. Minerals travel upwards through **xylem vessels**.
- **Sugars** travel from the **leaves** (where they are made by photosynthesis) to all parts of the plan through **phloem tubes**.

### Reproduction

- Many plants can reproduce **asexually** and **sexually**.
- During **sexual** reproduction **pollen** (the male gamete) is transferred to the **stigma** by wind or insects.
- A pollen tube grows and the pollen grain nucleus travels through this to join to the egg cell nucleus.
- A **seed** develops inside a **fruit** and is dispersed away from the parent plant.
- In the right conditions (water, oxygen, the correct temperature), seeds will **germinate** to develop into new plants.

### Hormones

- Plant growth and development is controlled by plant hormones.
- Farmers and gardeners can use plant hormones to control stages of the plant life cycle and increase crop production.

### REVISION ACTIVITY

1. Write the photosynthesis equation.

   _____ + _____ ⟶ _____ + _____

2. Label this diagram of a section through a leaf.

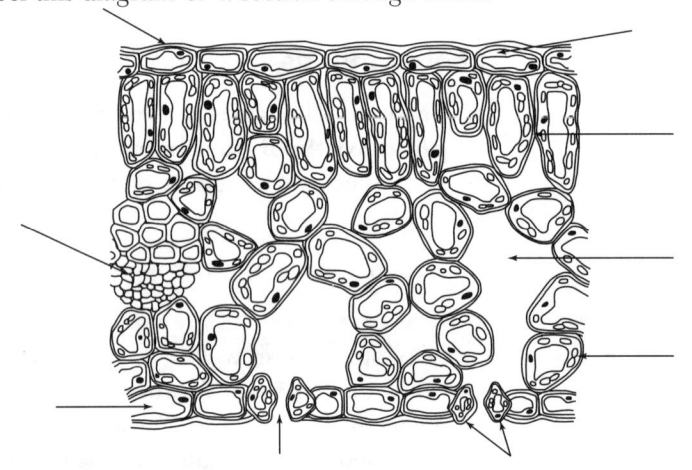

3. How are leaves adapted for photosynthesis?
4. Complete the table about leaf structure.

   | Part | Function |
   |------|----------|
   |      | most photosynthesis occurs here |
   |      | carries water to the leaf |
   |      | makes the waxy cuticle to protect the leaf |
   |      | pore to allow gases to enter and leave the leaf |
   |      | change shape to open and close the stomata |
   |      | carries sugar away from the leaf |

5. Fill in the gaps to complete the sentences about minerals.
   Plants get the minerals they need from the ____. They are absorbed by ____ transport and ____ in ____ cells which have a large ____ area. They travel upwards through ____ to all parts of the plant. Plants need a variety of minerals, including ____ to make protein and magnesium to make ____. If plants do not get the minerals they need, they will not grow properly and may look yellow. Farmers and gardeners can add extra minerals to the soil by digging in ____.

6. A leafy shoot was placed in a potometer, and the water loss was measured under different conditions by measuring how far the bubble moved along the scale in 5 minutes.

The experiment was carried out again, but with one surface of the leaves covered in Vaseline. Look at the results table and answer the questions that follow.

|  | Conditions | Distance bubble moved in 5 minutes (cm) |
|---|---|---|
| Shoot A (no Vaseline) | warm, light | 11.6 |
|  | warm, dark | 0.1 |
|  | cold, light | 7.2 |
|  | cold, dark | 0 |
| Shoot B (Vaseline on one surface of leaves) | warm, light | 0 |
|  | warm, dark | 0 |
|  | cold, light | 0 |
|  | cold, dark | 0 |

(a) In which conditions did transpiration occur fastest in Shoot A?
(b) Explain why.
(c) Name two other factors affecting transpiration rate.
(d) Calculate the distance the bubble moved per minute in cold, light conditions.
(e) Which leaf surface was covered in Vaseline in Shoot B, upper or lower? Explain your answer.

7  Look at this table about effects of plant hormones.

| Hormone | Effects |
|---|---|
| Auxins | 1  make plant shoot bend towards the light (phototropism)<br>2  make plant roots grow downwards in response to gravity (geotropism)<br>3  prevent leaves and fruits falling off plants<br>4  make roots develop<br>5  encourage fruit development |
| Gibberellins | 1  make plants grow taller<br>2  encourage germination of seeds<br>3  encourage fruit development<br>4  affect flowering time |
| Cytokinins | 1  increase growth rate<br>2  keep leaves healthy once plant is dug up<br>3  encourage germination of seeds |
| Abscissic acid | 1  slows down growth<br>2  makes leaves and fruits fall off<br>3  closes stomata |
| Ethene | 1  ripens fruit<br>2  causes flowering<br>3  encourages bud growth |

Which hormone would you use:
(a) as a synthetic rooting powder?
(b) to delay flowering?
(c) to ripen fruit?
(d) to stop lettuce leaves going yellow?
(e) to make it easier to harvest fruit?

# EXAMINATION QUESTIONS

### Question 1
(a) complete the equation for photosynthesis.

carbon dioxide + .................... ⟶ .................... + ....................   [3]

(b) The carbon dioxide enters the leaf via stomata which are found in the outer layer of the leaves. The drawing below shows a surface view of several stomata as seen through a microscope.

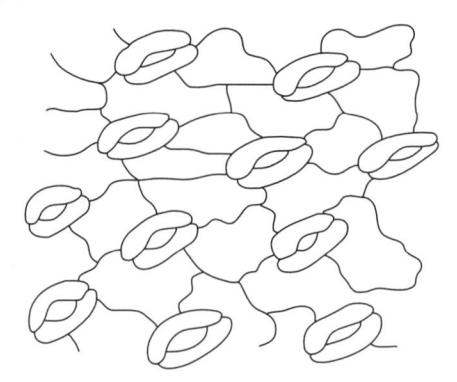

The area shown in the leaf is 0.01 mm square.
Calculate how many stomata there are in 1 mm² of the leaf surface.
(Show your working.) [2]
(c) Explain how stomata help to control the water content of the plant body. [2]

[NEAB]

## Question 2

(a) Fig. 1 shows the lower part of a section through the leaf of a flowering plant.

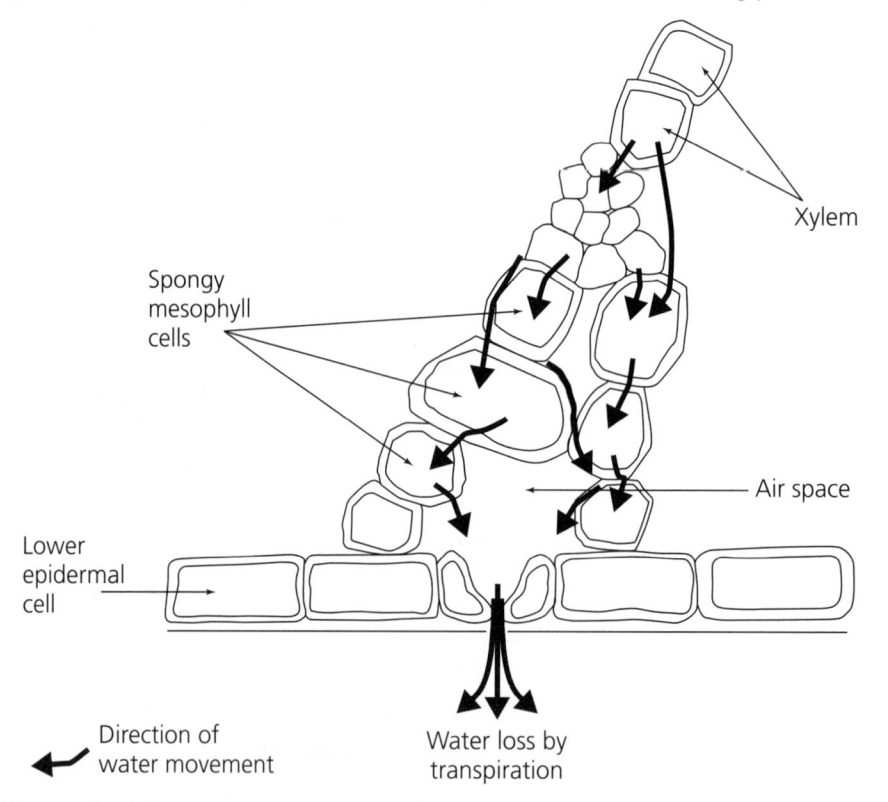

*Fig. 1*

(i) Not all of the water entering the leaf through the xylem is transpired through the stomata of the leaf. What happens to the water not transpired through the stomata? [2]
(ii) Describe briefly how you could show that the water present in the xylem is the same water that was absorbed by the roots of the plant. [3]
(iii) Name the support material, other than cellulose, present in the walls of the xylem vessels. [1]
(iv) The cell walls of the spongy mesophyll cells are little more than thin layers of cellulose. Describe how these cells support the leaf. [2]
(v) Describe how the loss of water vapour through the stomata contributes to the transport of materials from the roots to the leaves. [2]

(b) Fig. 2 is a graph showing the relative size of the stomatal openings over a 24-hour period for a flowering plant growing in a temperate climate in early summer.

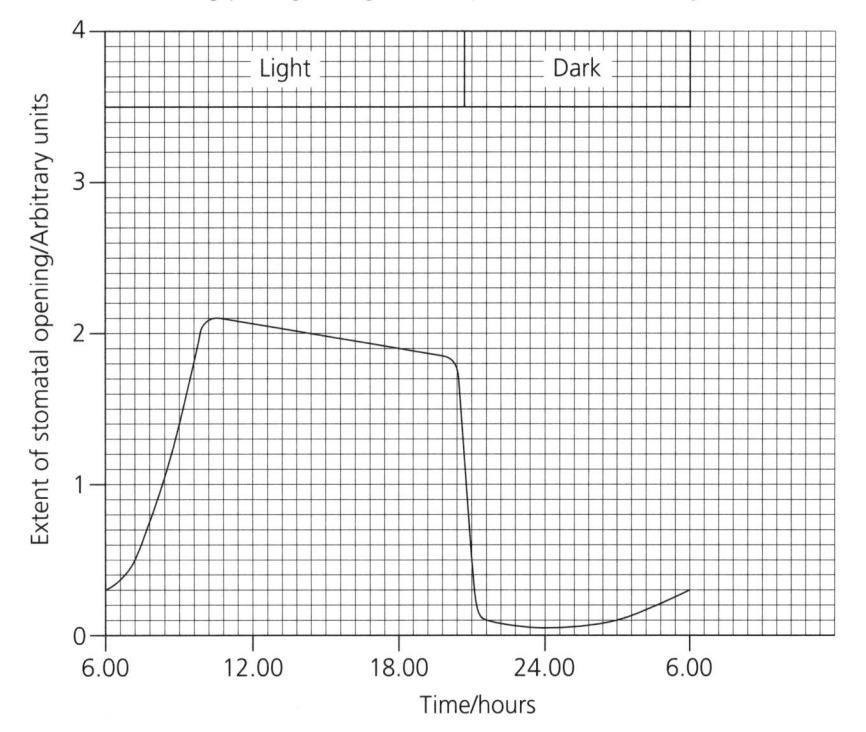

*Fig. 2*

(i) Using the data in Fig. 2, describe what happens to the stomatal openings during the 24-hour period. [5]
(ii) In temperate regions, temporary closure of the stomata may happen occasionally during daylight hours. Suggest an explanation for this fact. [2]
(iii) In the tropics, closure of stomata for a period around midday is very common. State ONE disadvantage and ONE advantage to the plant of this behaviour. [2]
(iv) Describe how osmosis may be involved in controlling the opening and closing of stomata. [5]

[MEG]

## Question 3
(a) The table below shows the results of an investigation to measure the mass of sugar in leaves at different times of the day.

| Time of day | Mass of sugar/g |
| --- | --- |
| 4.00 a.m. | 0.5 |
| 8.00 a.m. | 0.7 |
| 12 noon | 1.8 |
| 4.00 p.m. | 2.0 |
| 8.00 p.m. | 1.4 |
| 12 midnight | 0.6 |
| 4.00 a.m. | 0.5 |

(i) On the axes below, plot the results as a line graph. [4]
(ii) At what time of the day was the mass of sugar at a maximum in the leaf? Explain your answer. [2]
(iii) Explain why the mass of sugar fell between 8.00 p.m. and 12 midnight. [2]

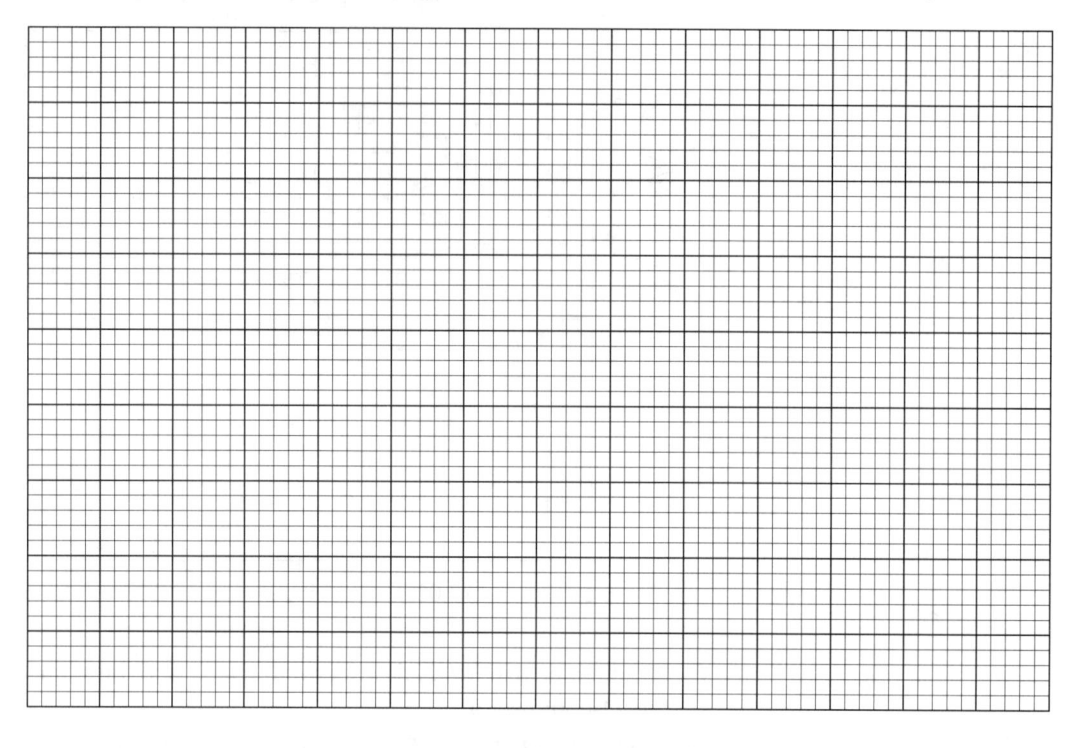

Mass of sugar (g)

Time of day

(b) A gardener grew plants in greenhouse as shown below.

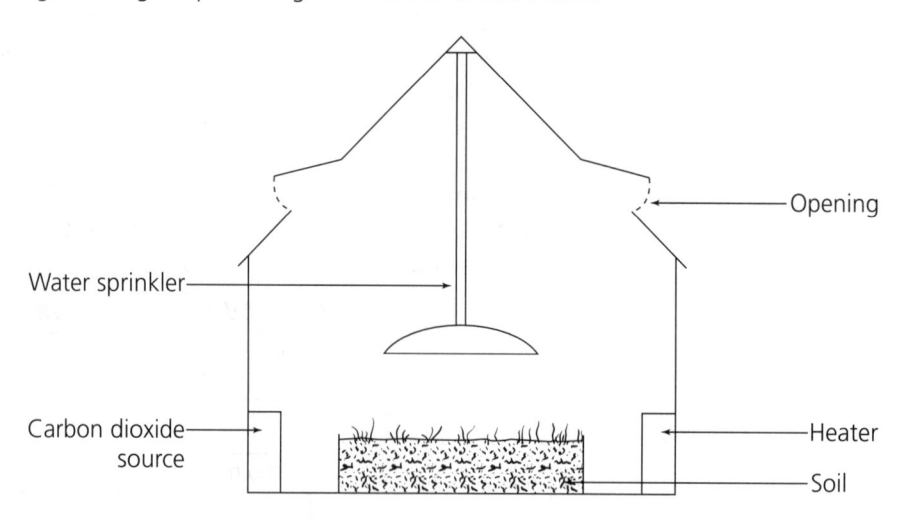

Opening
Water sprinkler
Carbon dioxide source
Heater
Soil

(i) Give TWO conditions in the greenhouse which could limit the rate of photosynthesis in the plants. [2]
(ii) Explain why the use of additional light may not lead to an increase in the growth of the plants. [2]

[NICCEA]

# 4 Variation, inheritance and evolution

## REVISION TIPS

This topic requires you to know the main features of groups of organisms (plants, vertebrates and invertebrates) and you should be able to use simple keys to identify unknown organisms.

Genetics problems form a large part of this topic. It is important that you can use genetic diagrams to show sex determination (with XX and XY chromosomes) and show how parents pass on features to their offspring (using genetic symbols, e.g. BB and Bb).

There are a lot of new words to learn and you should know the meaning of all of the following:

| | | |
|---|---|---|
| gene | diploid | genotype |
| chromosome | haploid | phenotype |
| allele | dominant | cloning |
| homozygous | recessive | mutation |
| heterozygous | | |

In the higher level paper, you are expected to know about the structure of DNA and its role in protein synthesis and about the techniques and implications of genetic engineering. Some of this work is quite challenging, but it is worth persevering so that you can answer questions testing your understanding as well as recall.

You should know about selective breeding and how cloning can be carried out to produce identical individuals. Data questions or comprehension questions are often set to test natural selection and evolution. Make sure you understand the basic principles so you can apply them to the information you are given.

## TOPIC OUTLINE

### Classification

- All living things are classified into **five** kingdoms: bacteria (monera), protoctists, fungi, plants and animals.
- **Plants** are classified into **four** main groups: mosses, ferns, conifers and flowering plants. You should know the main external features of each group.
- **Animals** are often classified as **invertebrates** or **vertebrates**.
  **Invertebrates** include insects, spiders, crustaceans, molluscs and segmented worms.
  **Vertebrates** include fish, amphibians, reptiles, birds and mammals.
  You should know the main external features of each group.

### Genes and variation

- Biologists use simple **keys** to identify unknown organisms. These may be **branching** keys or **number** keys.
- **Variation** means that individuals within a species are different to each other. It can be caused by **genes** (inherited from parents) or by the **environment**.

- A **gene** is a length of DNA carrying instructions about a particular feature of an individual. Genes are part of **chromosomes**, which are found in the nuclei of all cells.
- Genes exist in alternative forms called **alleles**, e.g. there is a gene for eye colour, with alleles for blue eyes, brown eyes, hazel eyes, etc.
- **Body cells** contain pairs of chromosomes, so they have two copies of each gene. This number of chromosomes is called the **diploid number** and in humans it is **46**.
- **Gametes** contain single chromosomes, so they have one copy of each gene. This number of chromosomes is called the **haploid number** and in humans it is **23** (the haploid number is always half of the diploid number).
- **Meiosis** (cell division) produces **haploid gametes**.
- When male and female gametes (both haploid) fuse at **fertilisation**, the **zygote** that is formed is **diploid**. It receives genes from both parents, so it inherits features from both parents.
- Two of the chromosomes are called **sex chromosomes**. Females are always **XX** and males are always **XY**.
- An individual's **phenotype** is their appearance or characteristics, e.g. blue eyes. Their **genotype** is the alleles they have, e.g. bb.
- If an individual has two identical alleles, we say they are **homozygous**, e.g. bb, or BB. If they have two different alleles, we say they are **heterozygous**, e.g. Bb.
- Some alleles are **dominant** to others (we normally show these with a capital letter symbol), and will always show in the phenotype.
  Other alleles are **recessive** (we use a lower case letter for these) and will only show in the phenotype if there are **two** of them,
  e.g.   BB – brown eyes,  Bb – brown eyes,  bb – blue eyes
       allele B is dominant, allele b is recessive.
- You must be able to draw simple genetic diagrams to show how features are inherited.
- Some **diseases** are caused by **faulty genes** and can be passed on from parents to children, e.g. cystic fibrosis, sickle cell anaemia, Huntington's chorea. In some cases, parents are carriers (heterozygous), e.g. Aa, and can pass on the allele for the disease, even though they have no symptoms themselves.
- Some conditions are **sex-linked**, because the allele is carried on the X chromosome, e.g. red-green colourblindness, haemophilia. Men suffer from these conditions much more often than women.
- Some alleles show **incomplete dominance** (co-dominance), where neither allele is dominant or recessive. In this case, both alleles will show equally in the phenotype, e.g. blood group AB individuals.

### DNA and protein synthesis

- **DNA** is found in the **nucleus** of all **cells**, and it carries genetic information in the form of a **genetic code**. It is a large molecule made of two strands of nucleotides twisted together – it is sometimes called a **double helix**. The strands are linked by bases which are matched together: **adenine** links to **thymine**, **cytosine** links to **guanine**.
- DNA carries information to make all the **proteins** in the body: one gene carries information to make one protein. Protein synthesis occurs in the **cytoplasm**, and the DNA must remain in the nucleus, so a copy of the gene is made from **RNA**. RNA passes out of the nucleus into the cytoplasm and acts as a template (pattern) for protein synthesis.
- The **genetic code** is the order of bases on the DNA (and its copy made from RNA). The bases are read in groups of three (a codon, or triplet) and

each group codes for a single amino acid. The correct amino acids are joined together in the correct order to make a protein.
- **Genetic engineering** means transferring DNA (a gene) from one organism to another, so that the recipient can make new proteins. The gene for insulin has been transferred from humans to bacteria, so that the bacteria can make insulin and this can be used by diabetics.
- **Cloning** means producing genetically identical offspring from a single parent. It may be **natural**, e.g. when yeasts or bacteria reproduce asexually, or when plants reproduce asexually with bulbs or runners.
  It may be **artificial**, e.g. when gardeners take plant cuttings or carry out micropropagation, or when embryos are split in animal breeding.
- **Selective breeding** (sometimes called artificial selection) is a way of choosing parents in order to obtain a particular type of offspring. It is important in the development of crop plants, e.g. for disease resistance or to get high yields, and in the development of domestic animals, e.g. breeds of dog, breeds of cattle.
- When a cell divides, the DNA must be **copied** so that the new cell gets a set of chromosomes. Sometimes the DNA is copied inaccurately and we say a **mutation** has occurred. This can happen naturally, but is increased by exposure to radiation and to some chemicals.

### Natural selection and evolution

- Mutations increase **variation**. They may be helpful or neutral, but are usually harmful to the organism.
- Due to variation, some individuals are better suited to their environment than others, so they are more likely to survive. They will breed and produce offspring like themselves: this process is called **natural selection**.
- Natural selection is most obvious when conditions are hostile, i.e. there is competition for resources, and the individuals who are not suited to the environment die out.
- Gradually, the features of the population change and the accumulation of changes over a long period of time is called **evolution**. The fossil record is incomplete, but it suggests that many species have evolved like this.

### REVISION ACTIVITY

1 Complete this table about the characteristics of vertebrates.

| Named example | Scales? | Feathers? | Fur? | Fins? | Legs? | Lay eggs? | Breathe air? |
|---|---|---|---|---|---|---|---|
| Fish | | | | | | | |
| Amphibians | | | | | | | |
| Reptiles | | | | | | | |
| Birds | | | | | | | |
| Mammals | | | | | | | |

2 Name an organism which matches each of the following descriptions.
   (a) Has no backbone, has eight legs and no antennae.
   b) Has simple leaves with xylem and phloem tubes, and spores on the underside of the leaves.
   (c) Has wings, six legs and three body parts (head, thorax, abdomen)
   (d) Has a backbone, lives in water but breathes air; gives birth to live babies.
   (e) Has no backbone and no legs. Has a soft body which may be protected by a shell.

**3** Use the key to identify the animal shown.

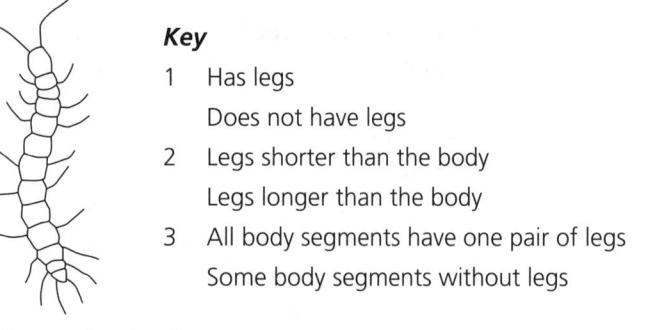

**Key**
1. Has legs — go to 2
   Does not have legs — Enchytraeid
2. Legs shorter than the body — go to 3
   Legs longer than the body — Lycosa
3. All body segments have one pair of legs — Geophilus
   Some body segments without legs — Scutigerella

Name of animal:

**4** (a) What does 'haploid' mean?
(b) Explain why gametes must be haploid.
(c) Which type of cell division produces haploid gametes?
(d) Complete this diagram by writing in the chromosome numbers for human cells.

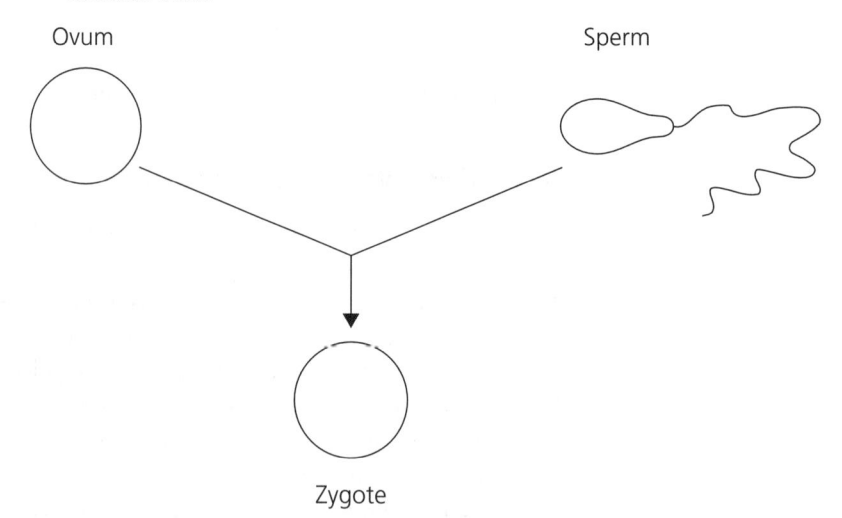

Ovum         Sperm

                Zygote

**5** Explain the differences between the following pairs of terms.
(a) chromosome and gene
(b) genotype and phenotype
(c) homozygous and heterozygous

**6** In pea plants, the allele for tall (T) is dominant to the allele for dwarf (t). Show what would occur if a heterozygous tall plant was crossed with a dwarf plant.

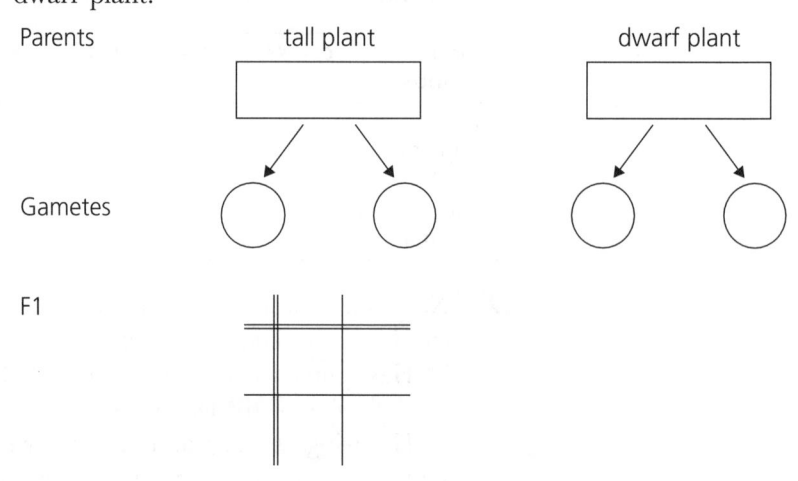

Parents        tall plant            dwarf plant

Gametes

F1

What are the phenotypes of the offspring?
What is the ratio of phenotypes?

# variation, inheritance and evolution

7. Some conditions are described as sex linked, e.g. red-green colourblindness. A woman who is a carrier for this condition ($X^R X^r$) marries a normal man ($X^R Y$) and they have one child.
   If it is a boy, what is the probability he is colourblind?
   If it is a girl, what is the probability she is colourblind?
   Make a genetic diagram to provide evidence for your answer.

8. Complete the diagram to show base pairing in DNA.

   Write out the names of the bases in full.
   A = _____
   G = _____
   T = _____
   C = _____

   Why is DNA called a double helix?

9. Fill in the spaces to complete this paragraph about natural selection and evolution.

   In any species, there is ____ between individuals, i.e. they are not all identical. This is partly due to the ____ they inherit from their parents and to mutation. Mutation is a mistake in copying ____ when the cell divides, and the chance of this happening is increased by ____, e.g. radiation or ____. When resources are scarce, individuals have to ____ to survive. Some individuals are better suited to their environment so they will survive, but others will ____. The survivors will ____ and will have offspring like themselves. Gradually, changes will build up and we say that ____ has occurred. One example of natural selection involves peppered moths which rest on lichen-covered tree trunks. In rural areas, the trunks are ____ coloured, so the moths are well camouflaged. In industrial areas, ____ have killed the lichens and the trunks are darkened by soot. Here pale moths are not well camouflaged, so they are eaten by ____. Mutant ____ moths are much more likely to survive.

## EXAMINATION QUESTIONS

### Question 1

Fig. 1, p.34, shows six different types of organisms.

(a) Living things can be classified into five kingdoms (Bacteria, Protoctists, Fungi, Plants and Animals). How many of these kingdoms are represented by the organisms in Fig. 1? [1]

(b) Use the key below to identify organism D. Give the order of numbers from the key which led to your answer.

**Key**

| | | |
|---|---|---|
| 1 | True roots present | go to 2 |
| | True roots not present | go to 4 |
| 2 | Produces flowers | Flowering plant |
| | Does not produce flowers | go to 3 |
| 3 | Young 'leaves' coiled in bud | Fern |
| | Needle-like leaves | Conifer |
| 4 | Plant has a large number of 'leaves' | Moss |
| | Leaves not present | go to 5 |
| 5 | Hyphae present; produces spores | Fungus |
| | Hyphae not present | Liverwort |

Answer................ Sequence................ [2]

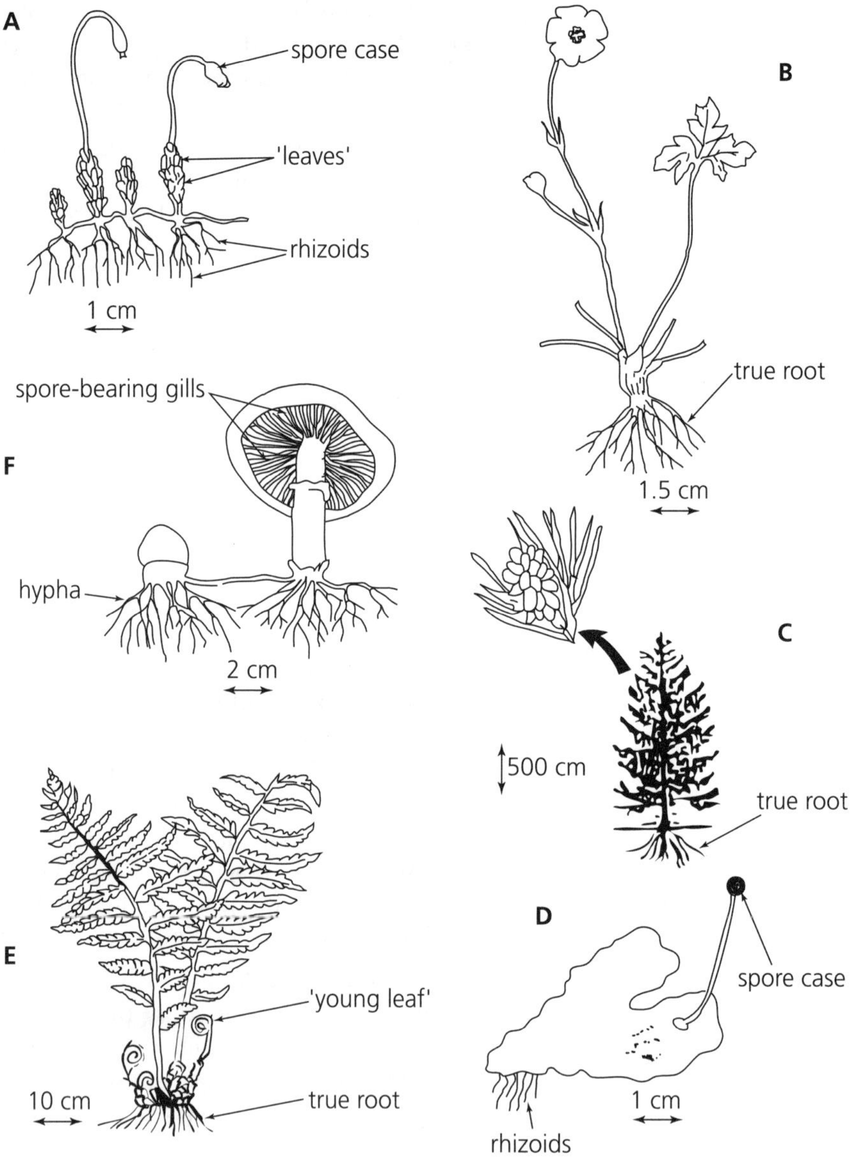
A
spore case
'leaves'
rhizoids
1 cm
B
true root
1.5 cm
spore-bearing gills
F
hypha
2 cm
C
500 cm
true root
E
'young leaf'
10 cm
true root
D
spore case
rhizoids
1 cm

*Fig. 1*

[MEG]

***Question 2***

(a) Complete the list below of the characteristics of living organisms.

1 Reproduction    4 ......................................
2 Sensitivity    5 ......................................
3 Nutrition    6 ......................................
    7 ...................................... [4]

(b) The table below gives some characteristics of four animal groups.

| ***Group*** | ***Example*** | ***Reproduction*** | ***Characteristics*** |
|---|---|---|---|
| Fish | Cod | External fertilisation<br>Many eggs laid in water | Fins<br>Scales |
| Amphibians | Frog | External fertilisation<br>Many eggs laid in water | Moist skin<br>Lungs in adult |
| Reptiles | Snake | Internal fertilisation<br>Small number of eggs laid on land | Scales<br>Lungs |
| Birds | Robin | Internal fertilisation<br>Small number of eggs laid on land<br>Parental care | Lungs<br>Beak |

## variation, inheritance and evolution 35

Use the information in the table to help answer the question below.
(i) Give TWO ways in which amphibians are similar to fish. [2]
(ii) Give THREE features of reptiles which help them live on land. Give an explanation for each. [6]
(iii) Name another feature, not given in the table, which is characteristic of each of the groups below.
Fish feature ..................................
Birds feature .................................. [2]
[NICCEA]

### Question 3
(a) The table below shows some examples of variation in 11-year-old pupils.

| Name | Can roll tongue | Height (cm) | Right/left handed | Shoe size |
| --- | --- | --- | --- | --- |
| Derek | Yes | 153 | Right | 38 |
| Sean | No | 159 | Right | 38 |
| Anne | Yes | 149 | Right | 36 |
| Siobhan | Yes | 151 | Right | 37 |
| Joe | No | 162 | Left | 39 |
| Angela | Yes | 152 | Right | 37 |
| Pascal | Yes | 163 | Right | 40 |
| Louise | Yes | 156 | Left | 38 |
| Robert | Yes | 161 | Right | 39 |
| Linda | No | 156 | Left | 36 |
| Kim | Yes | 154 | Right | 37 |
| Patrick | Yes | 165 | Right | 40 |

(i) What fraction of the pupils is
left handed? ........................ over 160 cm in height? ......................[2]
(ii) Give TWO examples of discontinuous variation shown in the table. [2]
(iii) Explain why some characteristics are described as showing continuous variation.[2]
(iv) Suggest how the information recorded in the table will have changed when the pupils have reached 15 years of age. [2]
(b) Variation may be caused by mutations.
(i) What is a mutation? [2]
(ii) Explain why a mutation in the sperm cells of a man could lead to increased variation in his children. [2]
[NICCEA]

### Question 4
(a) Complete the diagram to show how the sex of a child depends on the chromosomes the child inherits. [3]

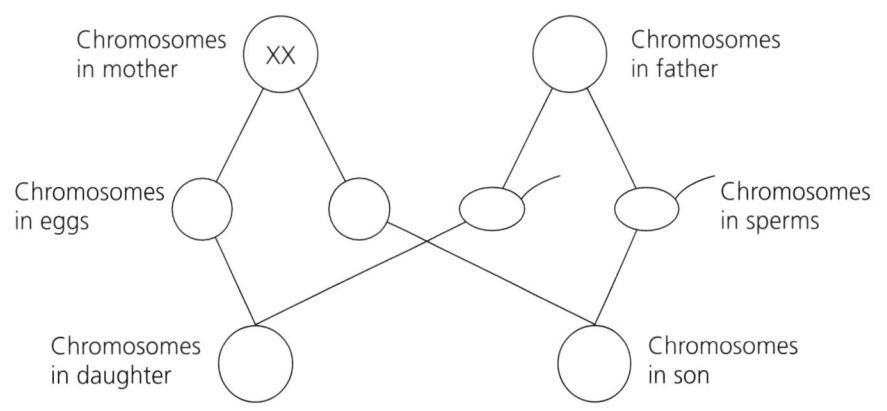

(b) The diagram shows the inheritance of Huntington's chorea in a family

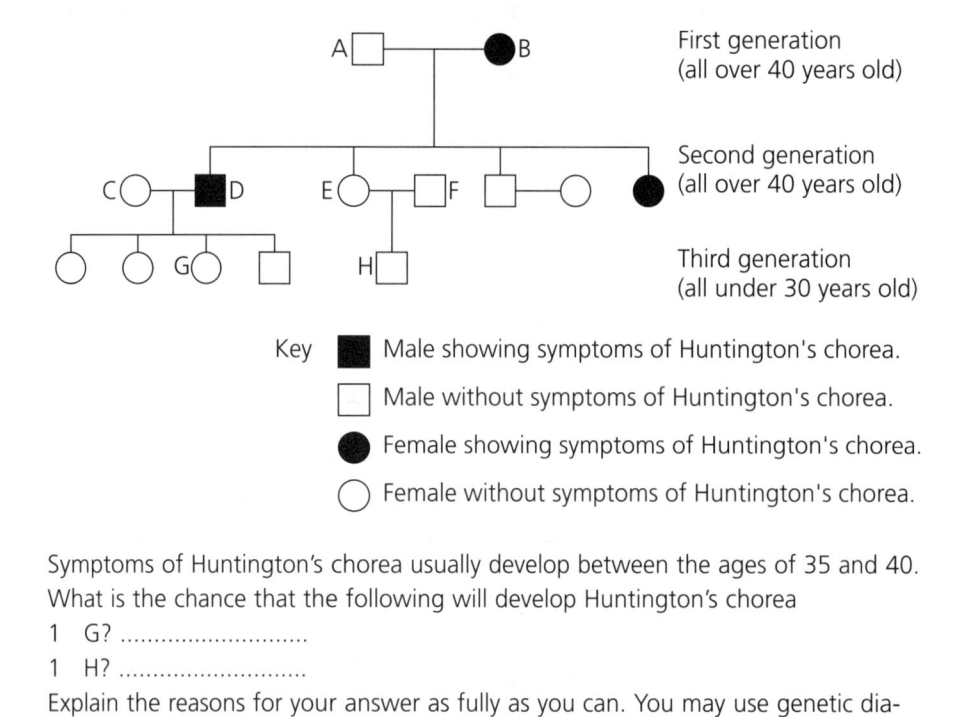

First generation (all over 40 years old)

Second generation (all over 40 years old)

Third generation (all under 30 years old)

Key
■ Male showing symptoms of Huntington's chorea.
□ Male without symptoms of Huntington's chorea.
● Female showing symptoms of Huntington's chorea.
○ Female without symptoms of Huntington's chorea.

Symptoms of Huntington's chorea usually develop between the ages of 35 and 40. What is the chance that the following will develop Huntington's chorea

1  G? .........................
1  H? .........................

Explain the reasons for your answer as fully as you can. You may use genetic diagrams if you wish. [6]

[NEAB]

## Question 5

The table below shows how three alleles control the ABO human blood group system.

| Allele | Effect |
|---|---|
| $I^A$ | Causes the production of antigen A on red blood cells |
| $I^B$ | Causes the production of antigen B on red blood cells |
| $I^O$ | Does not cause the production of antigen on red blood cells |

When $I^A$ and $I^B$ are inherited together they are equal in their effect. When $I^O$ is inherited with either $I^A$ or $I^B$ it is recessive.

(a) Complete the diagram below by filling in the blank circles to show the possible inheritance of the ABO blood group system in Mr and Mrs Smith's children. [3]

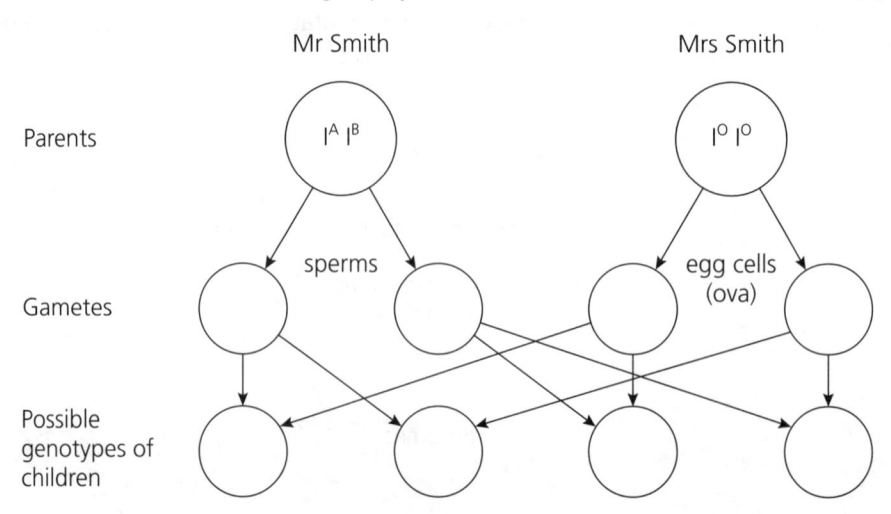

Mr Smith  Mrs Smith

Parents: $I^A I^B$    $I^O I^O$

Gametes: sperms     egg cells (ova)

Possible genotypes of children

(b) When $I^A$ and $I^B$ are inherited together they both show their effects in the phenotype. Name the term used to describe this. [1]
(c) (i) What is the probability of the eldest child being male? [1]
    (ii) What is the probability of the eldest child being male with blood group B? [1]

# variation, inheritance and evolution

(d) Sometimes a patient needs a blood transfusion. It is very important that the blood given to the patient does not contain any antigen which is not in the patient's own red blood cells. Which parent can donate blood safely to any of the possible children? [1]

**Total 7 marks**
[ULEAC]

## Question 6

(a) Haemophilia is a disease which prevents blood clotting properly.
Normal blood clotting is controlled by a dominant allele (H). The haemophiliac condition is controlled by the recessive allele (h).
The diagram below shows the sex chromosomes of a haemophiliac male, marking the position of the allele (h) responsible for the condition.
In the other box provided, draw the sex chromosomes and label the appropriate allele or alleles of a female carrier. [2]

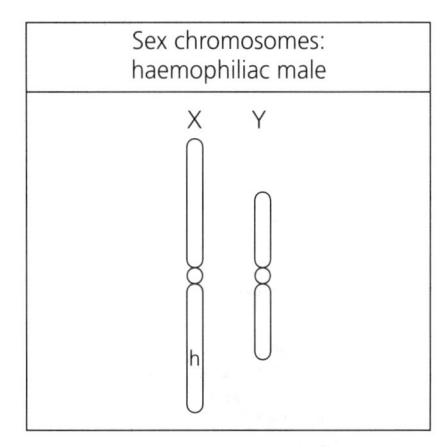

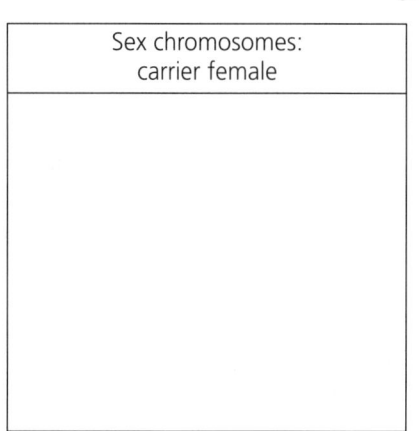

| Sex chromosomes: haemophiliac male | Sex chromosomes: carrier female |
|---|---|
| X Y (h marked on X) | |

(b) The family tree below shows some people with normal blood clotting, some who are haemophiliacs and others who are 'unknown' for this factor.

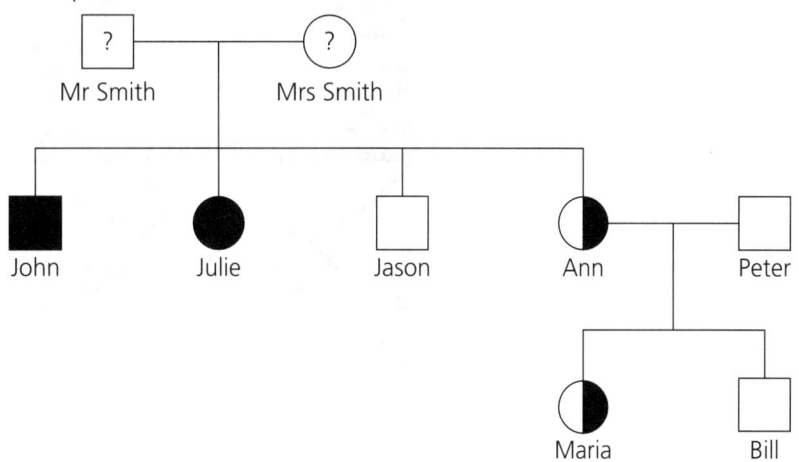

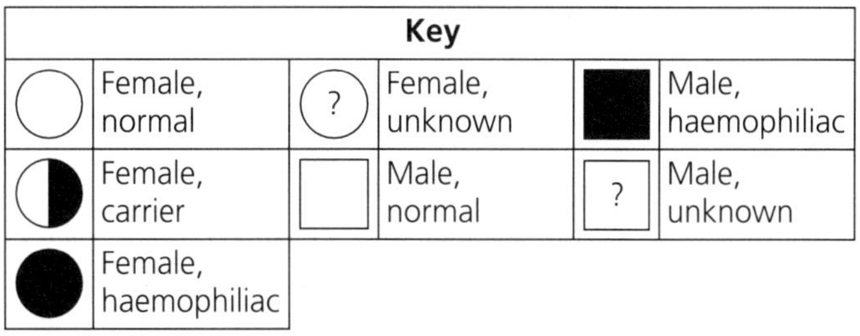

Mr Smith (?) — Mrs Smith (?)

Children: John (male haemophiliac), Julie (female haemophiliac), Jason (male unknown), Ann (female carrier) — Peter (male unknown)

Ann and Peter's children: Maria (female carrier), Bill (male unknown)

**Key**

| ○ | Female, normal | ? | Female, unknown | ■ | Male, haemophiliac |
|---|---|---|---|---|---|
| ◐ | Female, carrier | □ | Male, normal | ?□ | Male, unknown |
| ● | Female, haemophiliac | | | | |

Use the information in the diagram to answer the following questions.

(i) What are the genotypes for Mr and Mrs Smith?
Mr Smith .......................... Mrs Smith ..............................
Explain how you arrived at your answer. [4]

(ii) What is the probability of Ann and Peter producing a haemophiliac female? Explain how you arrived at your answer. [3]

(c) The diagram below shows chemicals produced by the body associated with the clotting process.

| No damage to blood vessels | Damage to blood vessels |
|---|---|
| Heparin in blood prevents clotting when there is no damage | Prothrombin and calcium ions<br>Thrombokinase produced by platelets → <br>Fibrinogen<br>Thrombin →<br>Fibrin (fibres which trap red blood cells) |

Suggest FOUR ways in which a faulty gene could affect the clotting process. [4]

**Total 13 marks**

[ULEAC]

## Question 7

The diagram below represents the behaviour of DNA strands during the early part of cell division.

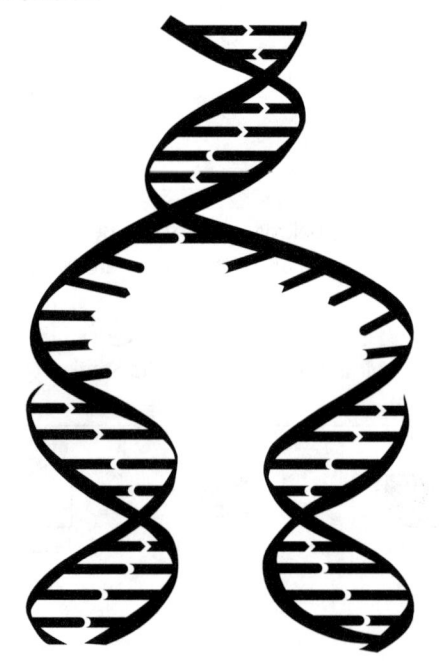

**Key**

| Organic base | Symbol |
|---|---|
| Adenine (A) | ▬▶ |
| X | ▬◀ |
| Y | ▬▬ |
| Guanine (G) | ▬◁ |

Use the information in the diagram to help you answer the following questions.

(a) Identify the organic bases X and Y. [2]
(b) Name and describe, in detail, the process shown in the diagram. [6]
(c) What is the importance of the SEQUENCE of organic bases along a DNA strand? [3]

**Total 11 marks**

[ULEAC]

## Question 8

(a) Domestic animals and cultivated plants can be improved by selective breeding.
 (i) Describe the process of selective breeding. [3]
 (ii) State **two** characteristics a farmer could improve in his wheat crop by selective breeding. [2]
(b) Tall, high-yielding tomato plants are deliberately crossed with short, disease-resistant tomato plants.

## variation, inheritance and evolution

The genotype of the tall plant is HH and that of the short plant is hh. The dominant allele is H.
  (i) Write down the genotype of the $F_1$ generation plants. [1]
  (ii) What proportion of the $F_1$ generation plants would be tall? [1]
  (iii) The $F_1$ generation plants are allowed to self-pollinate. The seeds from this cross are grown. State and explain the probable proportions of tall and short plants in the offspring. [3]
  (iv) The $F_1$ hybrid plant is very popular with tomato growers.
   Suggest **one** reason why commercial tomato growers may prefer to grow $F_1$ plants rather than the freely pollinated ones. [1]
  (v) A gardener grows twelve of the F1 hybrid seedlings. The seeds are all grown in the same conditions. Eleven of the plants are normal but one has white leaves. Suggest how this could have occurred. [2]
  (vi) Suggest and explain what will happen to the white-leaved seedling. [2]
(c) Genetic engineers can be successful in changing the characteristics of some plants and animals. Scientists are trying to transfer the nitrogen-fixing ability associated with plants such as peas into other crops such as cereals.
  (i) Describe how the characteristics of an organism can be changed by genetic engineering. [3]
  (ii) Suggest **two** advantages of having cereal crops which are nitrogen-fixing. [2]
  (iii) In developing new varieties of plant by genetic engineering, what danger should scientists be aware of and what precautions should they take? [3]

[MEG]

## Question 9

Flow chart 1 below shows, in the correct order, the principles of one technique used to improve crop plants by genetic engineering.

Table 2 lists the stages in the genetic engineering of cotton but they are listed in the **wrong** order. Write a letter (**A**, **B**, **C**, **D**, **E** or **F**) in each empty box in Flow chart 1 to match each principle with a stage. [6]

**Flow chart 1**

| Principles of genetic engineering | Box |
|---|---|
| A useful gene is identified | ☐ |
| ↓ | |
| This gene is cut out of the donor DNA | ☐ |
| ↓ | |
| The gene is inserted into a vector organism | ☐ |
| ↓ | |
| The vector transfers the useful gene to a cell of a crop plant | ☐ |
| ↓ | |
| The crop plant cell is cloned to produce many transgenic plants | ☐ |
| ↓ | |
| The new transgenic crop plants undergo trials to find out if the useful gene has the desired effect | ☐ |

**Table 2**

| Stages in the genetic engineering of cotton | Letter |
|---|---|
| Cotton plants of the new variety are tested in the field to find out if they kill insect pests | A |
| *Agrobacterium tumefaciens* infects cotton plant cells, passing the gene which controls toxin production into their nuclei | B |
| Whole cotton plants are grown from the genetically changed cotton plant cell | C |
| *Bacillus thuringiensis*, a bacterium, has a gene which controls the production of an insect-killing toxin | D |
| The gene controlling toxin production is transferred to *Agrobacterium tumefaciens*, a bacterium | E |
| The useful gene is cut from the bacterial DNA using an enzyme | F |

[ULEAC]

# 5 Living organisms in their environment

## REVISION TIPS

This topic covers the practical and theoretical aspects of ecology. You should know about the range of natural habitats, e.g. marine, freshwater, woodland, etc., and how organisms are adapted to survive in them. Population size depends on a variety of factors, e.g. competition, predation, environmental conditions, and you should be able to analyse data relating to this.

You should be able to explain how human activities affect organisms and their environment, e.g. pollution, farming, fishing and industrialisation. You could be given data questions, comprehension passages or extended prose questions on human impact on the environment – it is a very topical issue!

Food webs, food chains and biological pyramids, e.g. pyramids of numbers and biomass are commonly tested and higher level papers often have calculations on energy flow through ecosystems. Make sure that you understand the concept of energy transfer and that you learn the key stages of the carbon and nitrogen cycles.

You must be able to define these key words:

| population | ecosystem | secondary consumer |
| community | decomposer | herbivore |
| habitat | producer | carnivore |
| environment | primary consumer | trophic level |

Higher level papers may contain questions on the use of agricultural chemicals, e.g. pesticides, herbicides, fertilisers, and their effect on the environment. Be prepared to contrast these with organic farming methods, e.g. biological control and use of compost or manure.

## TOPIC OUTLINE

### Ecology

- A **population** is all the individuals of one species living in the same place, e.g. a population of limpets in a rock pool.
  A **community** is made up of individuals from different species in the same place, e.g. a rock pool community includes limpets, mussels, fish, seaweed, sea anemones.
- The **habitat** is the place where an organism lives, e.g. rock pool habitat, pond habitat, woodland habitat.
  The **environment** describes the type of habitat, and the conditions which exist there, e.g. temperature, rainfall, amount of light, type of soil, etc.
- The **ecosystem** is all of the living and non-living things in a habitat. It is the interaction between organisms and their environment.
- Organisms must be **adapted** (suitable) to live in a particular environment, otherwise they will not survive, e.g. fish have gills to absorb oxygen from water, polar bears have thick fur to keep them warm.
- Organisms compete for resources, e.g. food, space, light, water. Some organisms will not be successful and will die, others will survive and breed.

- The numbers of **predators** and **prey** are closely linked. If there are too many predators, the prey will be hunted too much and may die out, so then the predators would starve. If there are too few predators, prey numbers will increase (because they are not being eaten).
- **Population size** depends on conditions in the environment, competition and predation.
- Population size can be estimated during fieldwork by **sampling** in the environment.
  In aquatic environment use nets and collecting jars.
  In terrestrial environments use quadrats for plants; use nets, pitfall traps or mammal traps for animals.

## Humans and the environment

- Human activities change the natural environment, e.g. building, farming, fishing, mining, industry. They may destroy natural habitats, or may pollute the environment.
- Many fuels cause **air pollution** when they are burned. **Acid rain** is caused by **sulphur dioxide**, mainly from burned coal. Car exhaust gases include **carbon monoxide** and **nitrogen oxides**. **Carbon dioxide** is produced when any fuel is burned and high levels of this gas are linked to the **greenhouse effect**.
- Water is polluted by human sewage and by farm waste, e.g. fertilisers containing nitrates and phosphates which are washed into rivers. This can have serious effects on aquatic organisms, e.g. **eutrophication**.
- As the human population increases in size, and it becomes more industrialised and dependent on machines, the impact on the environment increases. There are several reasons for this, e.g. more land is needed for housing, roads and growing food; more fuel is needed for industry, houses and transport, so more air pollution occurs; more waste products are made, and these must be disposed of.

## Transfer of nutrients and energy

- **Food chains** show the feeding patterns of organisms in a habitat. They always start with a **producer** (plant); this is eaten by a **primary consumer** (herbivore), which in turn is eaten by a **secondary consumer** (carnivore). The last organism in a food chain is called the **top carnivore**. The different steps in a food chain are called **trophic levels**.
- A **pyramid of numbers** is a scale diagram showing the number of organisms at each trophic level of a food chain.
- A **pyramid of biomass** is a scale diagram showing the mass of organisms at each trophic level of a food chain.
- **Energy** for food chains comes from the **Sun** and is transferred along the food chain as one organism eats another. The amount of energy available for transfer decreases as you progress along the food chain, because each organism uses some of the energy to stay alive.
- Each **trophic level** of a food chain contains **less energy** than the previous level, and contains **less biomass** than the previous level. This accounts for the triangular shape of a pyramid of biomass.
- **Decay** occurs when organisms called **decomposers** (bacteria and fungi) feed on dead organic material, e.g. dead organisms or their waste products. Decay occurs fastest when it is warm and damp with plenty of air.
- The element **carbon** is found in carbon dioxide and in carbohydrates, protein and fats; the **carbon cycle** describes how it can be changed from one form to another in the environment.

Plants use carbon dioxide to make carbohydrate (during photosynthesis).
Animals and plants change carbohydrate into carbon dioxide (during respiration).
Decomposers release carbon dioxide in the process of decay.
- The element **nitrogen** is found in the air, and in proteins and other compounds inside living things; the **nitrogen cycle** describes how it can be changed from one form to another in the environment. Bacteria are very important in the nitrogen cycle.
Nitrogen-fixing bacteria change nitrogen gas into nitrate in the soil.
Plants can use nitrate to make proteins.
Decomposers change proteins and waste products into ammonium compounds.
Nitrifying bacteria change ammonium compounds into nitrate in the soil.
Denitrifying bacteria change nitrate into nitrogen gas.
- Efficient food production depends on efficient energy transfer and control of pests and diseases. In agriculture or fish farming, the aim is to control the ecosystem so that the crop organism (animal or plant) gives the highest possible food yield.

## REVISION ACTIVITY

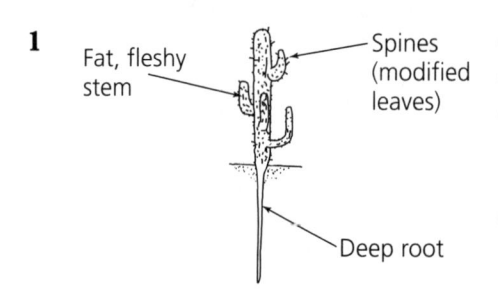

**1** Cacti are adapted to live in desert environments.
  (a) State two features of a desert ecosystem which may make survival difficult.
  (b) Explain how the adaptations labelled on the diagram will help this plant to survive.

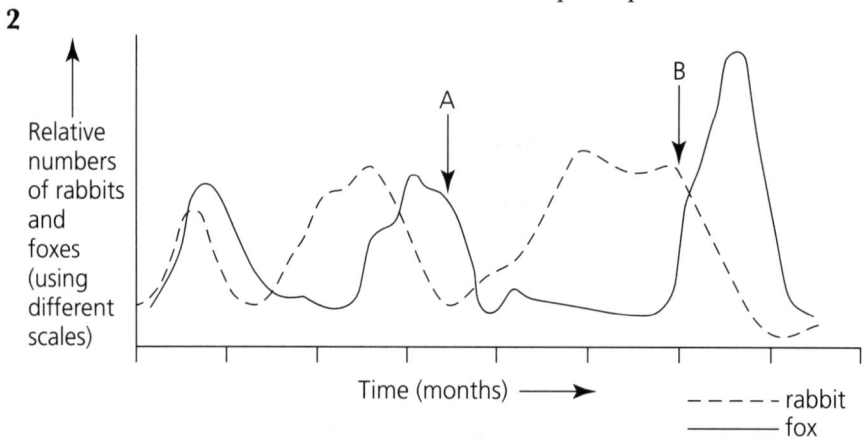

*Labels on diagram: Fat, fleshy stem; Spines (modified leaves); Deep root*

**2** Look at the graph for population numbers of foxes and rabbits.
  (a) Which animal is the predator?
  (b) Explain why the number of foxes decreased at point A.
  (c) Explain why the number of rabbits decreased at point B.
  (d) What would happen to the number of foxes if a lot of rabbits died from myxomatosis (a disease)? Explain why.

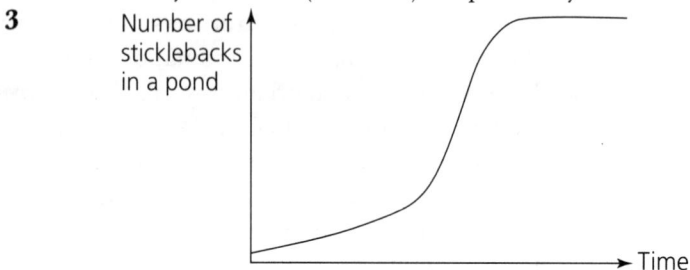

**3** *Graph showing number of sticklebacks in a pond vs time (S-shaped curve)*

The graph shows the number of sticklebacks in a small pond.
(a) Give two limiting factors which could cause the growth curve to level out like this.
(b) Add a line to the diagram to show what would happen to the population if three perch were added to the pond.
(c) Name two factors which could decrease the number of sticklebacks.

4  Many human activities cause pollution.
Name the pollutant or activity most closely associated with each of the situations in the following list. Choose from the words in the box.

| | | |
|---|---|---|
| oil pollution | carbon monoxide | sulphur dioxide |
| CFC's | carbon dioxide | dumping of untreated sewage |
| fertiliser run-off | accumulation of pesticides | |

(a) acid rain _____
(b) incompletely burned fossil fuels _____
(c) damage to the ozone layer _____
(d) eutrophication in fresh water _____
(e) death to seabirds and marine animals from poisoning or hypothermia _____
(f) the greenhouse effect and global warming _____
(g) top carnivores harmed by pollutant residues in the food they have eaten _____
(h) risk of disease to swimmers _____

5

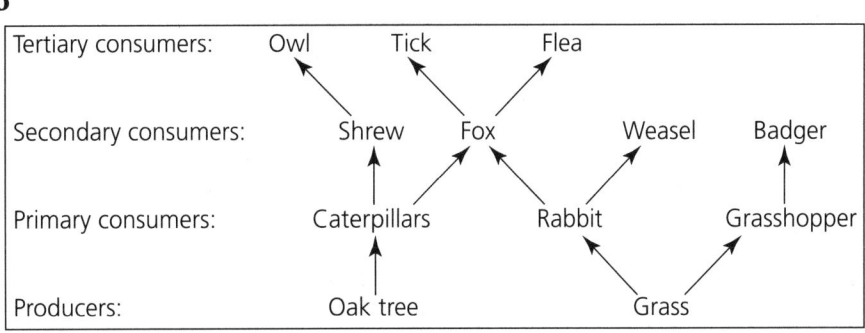

```
Tertiary consumers:     Owl      Tick      Flea

Secondary consumers:   Shrew   Fox      Weasel    Badger

Primary consumers:      Caterpillars   Rabbit    Grasshopper

Producers:              Oak tree       Grass
```

Look at the food web.
(a) Name the habitat this web comes from.
(b) Name one
   (i) producer      (ii) herbivore          (iii) top carnivore
   (iv) parasite     (v) primary consumer    (vi) secondary consumer
(c) Where does the energy for this food web come from?

6  (a) Which pyramid of numbers matches this food chain?
    oak tree → caterpillars → shrews → owl → fleas

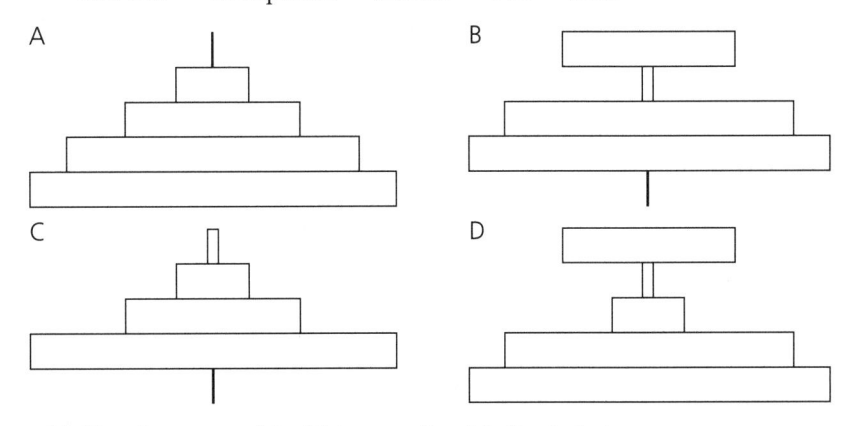

A                              B

C                              D

(b) Sketch a pyramid of biomass for this food chain.

**7**

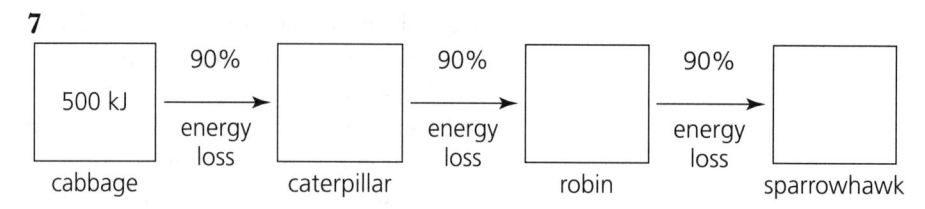

cabbage [500 kJ] →(90% energy loss)→ caterpillar [ ] →(90% energy loss)→ robin [ ] →(90% energy loss)→ sparrowhawk [ ]

In this food chain, the total energy in the green plant is shown in the box.
(a) Complete the other boxes to show the amount of energy in the tissues of the caterpillar, robin and sparrowhawk.
(b) Explain why only 10% of the energy is passed on at each stage.
(c) What does this tell you about the biomass of organisms at each trophic level?

**8** A group of students carried out an experiment to find out about conditions needed for decay. They took eight equal samples of food waste (bread, apple and yogurt) and placed them in different conditions for one week. Complete the table to show whether decay would have been fast, slow or not occurred at all, and give a reason for your choice.

| | light | wet | air available | temperature | decay fast/slow /not at all | reason |
|---|---|---|---|---|---|---|
| 1 | yes | yes | no | 25°C | | |
| 2 | yes | no | yes | 25°C | | |
| 3 | no | yes | yes | 25°C | | |
| 4 | yes | yes | yes | 10°C | | |
| 5 | yes | yes | yes | 2°C | | |
| 6 | no | no | yes | 37°C | | |
| 7 | yes | yes | no | 37°C | | |
| 8 | no | no | no | 37°C | | |

**9** Which processes are occurring at stages A, B, C, D and E in the carbon cycle?

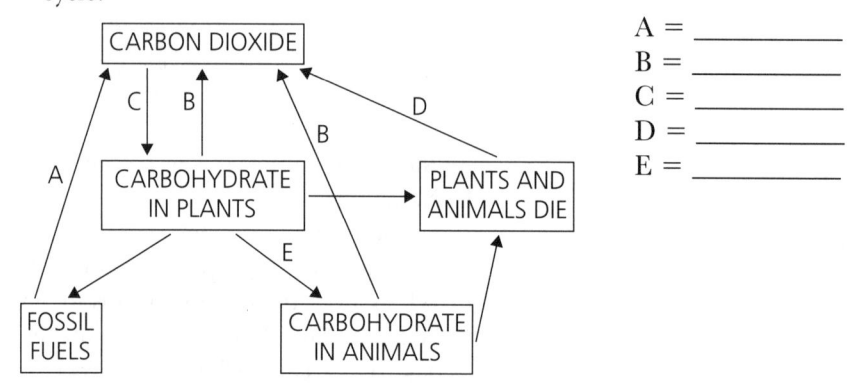

A = _____
B = _____
C = _____
D = _____
E = _____

**10** Complete these sentences to describe the nitrogen cycle.
Although the air is made up of 79% _____ gas, most organisms cannot use it. _____ bacteria live in root _____ of some plants, e.g. peas and _____, or they live free in the soil, and they can change _____ into nitrates. Nitrates are absorbed by plant roots, and used inside plants to make _____. When plants are eaten by _____, proteins containing nitrogen are transferred. Dead animals and plants and their waste products, e.g. urine, faeces, are broken down by _____ to form ammonium compounds. _____ bacteria change ammonium compounds into nitrates which plants can use. Farmers can add extra nitrate to the soil by digging _____ into it.

**11** Some farmers grow plants in large greenhouses so that they can control conditions to obtain a high crop yield.

### living organisms in their environment

State four conditions farmers would want to control and give a reason for each.
Why do farmers sometimes keep bees or other insects in greenhouses?

## EXAMINATION QUESTIONS

### Question 1
Ann saw a lot of holes in the leaves of some plants in her garden. She thought that the damage was caused by slugs. There was more damage in the vegetable garden than in the flower garden. She tried to find out if there were more slugs in the vegetable garden than in the flower garden.

Ann placed five pitfall traps for slugs in the flower garden and five in the vegetable garden. The diagrams below show the structure of a pitfall trap and a plan of Ann's garden.

A pitfall trap

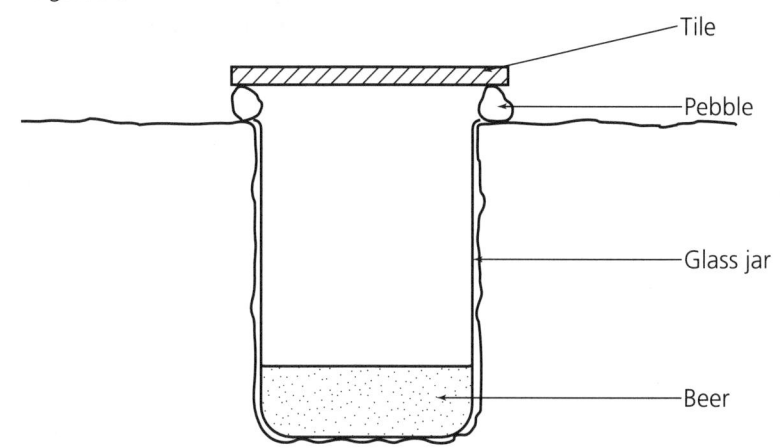

A plan of Ann's garden

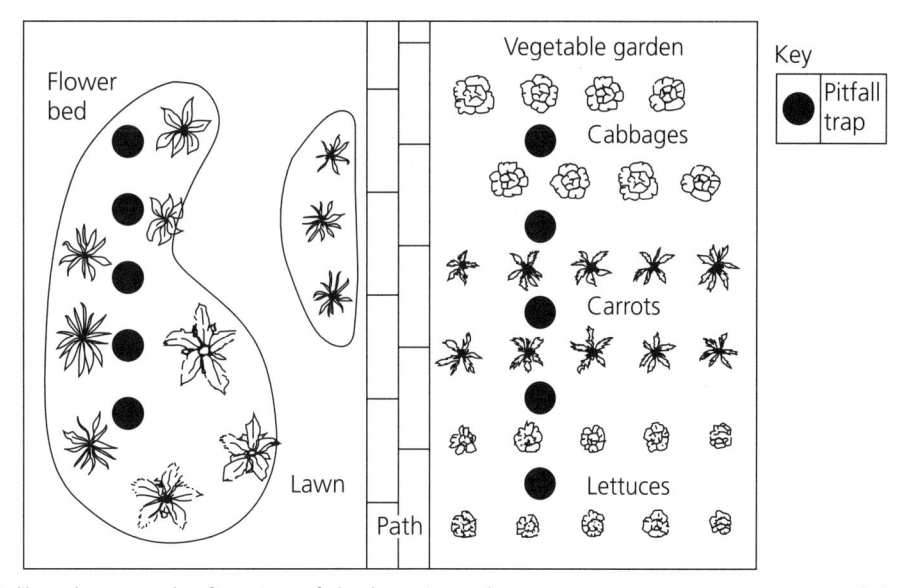

(a) (i) What was the function of the beer in each trap? [1]
(ii) Why was it important to use jars with slippery sides? [1]
(iii) Suggest TWO reasons why a tile was placed over each trap. [2]

The traps were left for 3 days. Ann then counted the slugs in each trap. The results are shown in the table below.

|  | Flower garden | Vegetable garden |
| --- | --- | --- |
| Number of slugs in each trap | 6　4　10　5　0 | 0　10　14　5　26 |

(b) The average number of slugs per trap in the flower garden was five.
What was the average number of slugs per trap in the vegetable garden?
Show your working. [2]

(c) (i) Suggest ONE explanation for the difference in the numbers of slugs in the flower and vegetable gardens. [1]
   (ii) How could you try to show if your explanation is correct? [1]
(d) Why was it a good idea to use more than one pitfall trap in each part of the garden? Give evidence from the table to support your answer. [2]
(e) Suggest ONE way in which Ann could improve her investigation. [1]

**Total 11 marks**
[ULEAC]

## Question 2

Untreated sewage from a farm was emptied into a river. A pupil took equal volumes of river water at various distances down stream from the sewage outflow. The amount of oxygen in each sample was measured and the animals were counted. Here are the results:

| Distance from sewage outflow (in metres) | % dissolved oxygen | Animals present |
|---|---|---|
| 0 | 0 | 20 rat-tailed maggots  36 sludgeworms |
| 20 | 3 | 8 rat-tailed maggots  20 sludgeworms |
| 50 | 10 | 2 rat-tailed maggots  5 sludgeworms |
| 100 | 25 | 5 sludgeworms  46 water lice |
| 150 | 50 | 40 water lice |
| 200 | 54 | 24 water lice  2 fish (sticklebacks) |

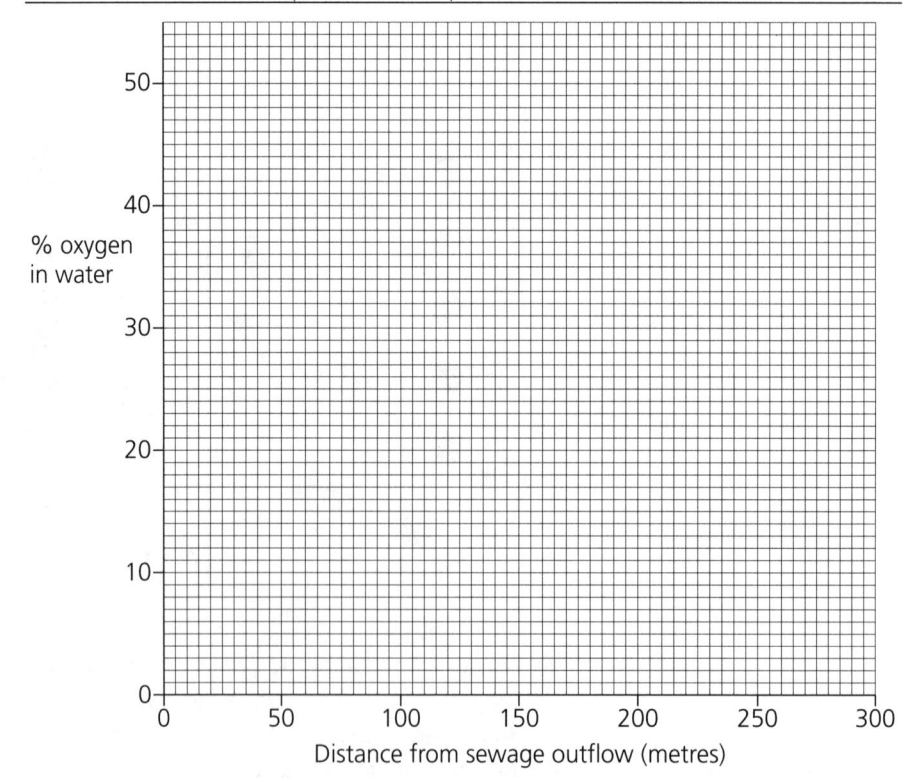

(a) On the grid, draw a line graph for oxygen in the water against distance from the sewage outflow. Join the points on the graph. [3]
(b) State what happens to the oxygen concentration in the water as it flows away from the outflow. [1]
(c) What would you expect the percentage of oxygen in the water to be at 125 m from the sewage outflow? [1]

(d) Which animal found in this survey appears to need **most** oxygen to survive? [1]
(e) (i) Name a type of organism in the sewage which alters the oxygen content.
(ii) What process causes this effect?
(iii) At what distance from the outflow would you find **most** of these organisms? [3]
(f) The diagram shows a rat-tailed maggot living in water.

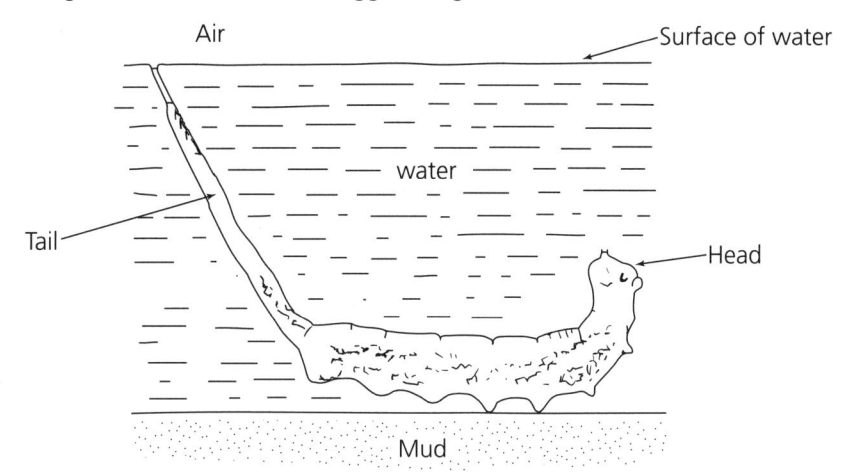

From the diagram suggest how the rat-tailed maggot can survive with such a low level of dissolved oxygen. [1]
(g) Here is a typical food chain for a clean river:
Microscopic algae ⟶ Water fleas ⟶ Insects ⟶ Sticklebacks
(i) What is shown by the **direction** of the arrows?
(ii) Which of these living things is likely to be present in **greatest** numbers?
(iii) What would you expect to happen to the numbers of microscopic algae if the numbers of insects suddenly increased? [3]

[WJEC]

## Question 3

(a) Farmers can control pests by using biological methods and by using chemical pesticides. Describe THREE advantages of using biological control organisms rather than pesticides. [3]

Read the following information and answer questions (b) (i) to (iv).

Lichens and bryophytes are plants which are very sensitive to atmospheric sulphur dioxide. Therefore they can be used as indicators of pollution levels. A survey of Newcastle-upon-Tyne in 1970 showed sulphur dioxide levels to be 65 micrograms per cubic metre of air in the western outskirts and 200 micrograms per cubic metre in the city centre. Fig. 1 shows the total number of species of lichens and bryophytes and the numbers of species growing in particular places at different distances from the city centre westwards. Sulphur dioxide is an acid gas.

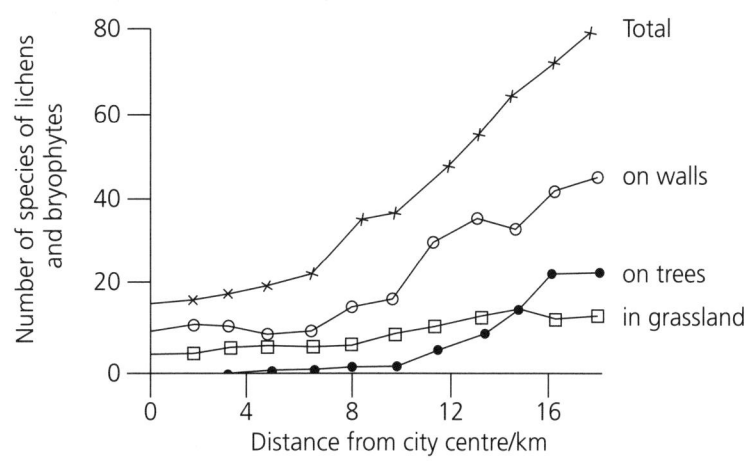

Fig. 1

(b) (i) To which atmospheric pollutant are lichens particularly sensitive? [1]
   (ii) What was the difference in sulphur dioxide level between the centre of Newcastle-upon-Tyne and its western outskirts in 1970? Show your working. [3]
   (iii) At what distance from the city centre did lichens and bryophytes first appear on trees in the city? [1]
   (iv) Brick walls are held together by mortar which contains lime. Lime is alkaline. Suggest how this might help to explain the figures given for the number of species of lichens and bryophytes growing on walls in the city. [2]

[MEG]

## Question 4

The diagram below shows a food web for a wood.

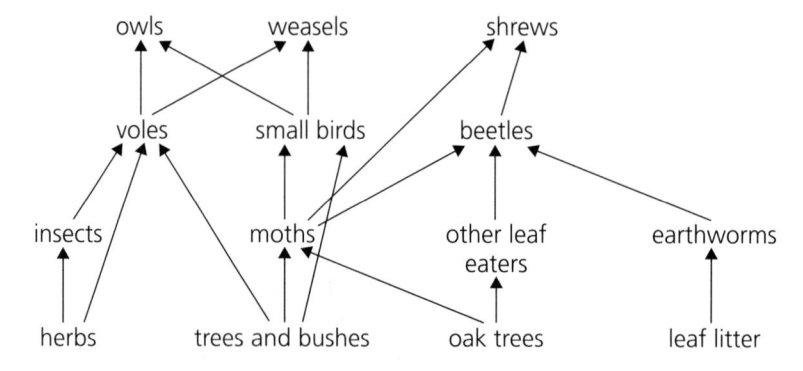

owls   weasels   shrews
voles   small birds   beetles
insects   moths   other leaf eaters   earthworms
herbs   trees and bushes   oak trees   leaf litter

(a) Construct a food chain which contains **four** organisms including shrews. [2]

(b) Explain what would happen to the populations of small birds and moths if the gamekeeper succeeds in catching some of the weasels. [4]

(c) The diagrams below show a pyramid of numbers and a pyramid of biomass for 0.1 hectare of this wood.

Pyramid of Numbers
numbers/0.1 hectare

2
120 000 — X
150 000
200 —
Y

Pyramid of Biomass
biomass (grams per square metre)

1
2
5139

(i) Name **one** organism from the level labelled X. [1]
(ii) Explain, as fully as you can, why the level labelled Y is such a different width in the two pyramids. [3]

(d) A 1 m² area of the floor of the wood was fenced off so that animals could not reach it. The graph shows the depth of leaf litter inside the fenced area over the next few months.

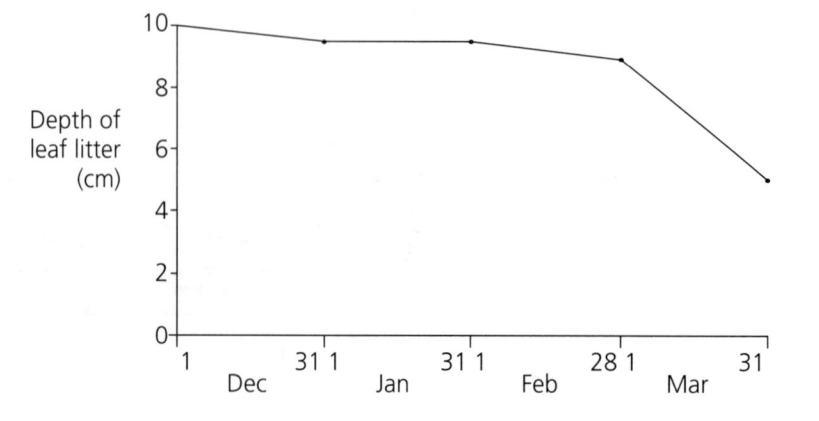

(i) Explain, as fully as you can, why and how the leaf litter gradually disappeared. [2]
(ii) In which month does leaf litter disappear fastest? Explain why. [2]
(iii) Explain, as fully as you can, how nitrogen from the protein molecules in the leaf litter eventually becomes part of the protein molecules of new leaves. [6]

[NEAB]

## Question 5

The diagram below represents the energy flow through a food web in a pond during one year.

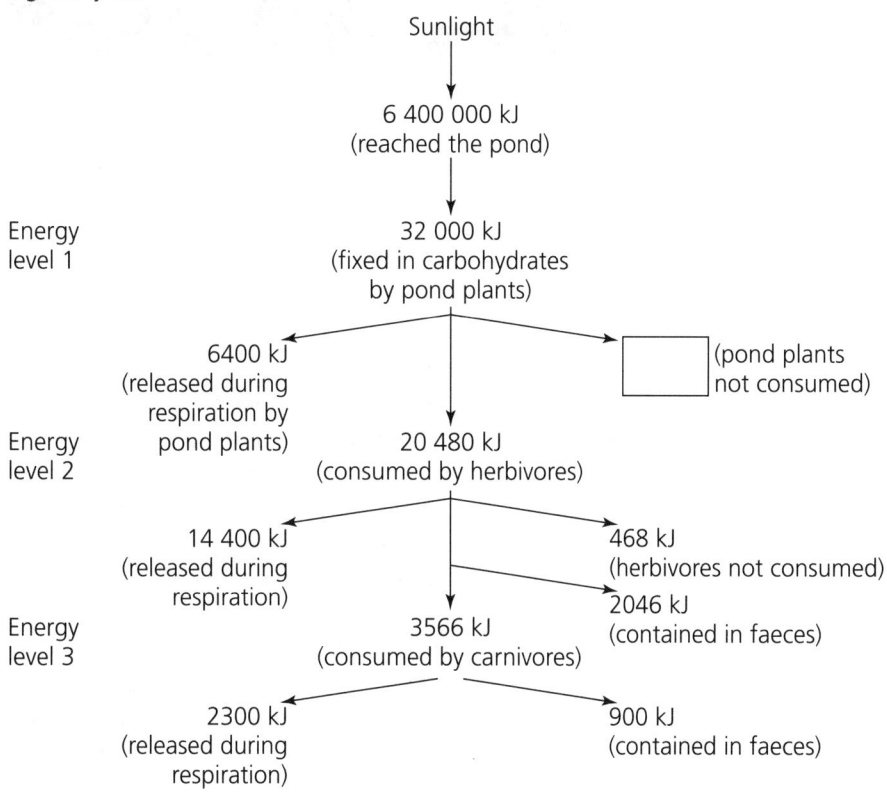

Sunlight
↓
6 400 000 kJ
(reached the pond)
↓
Energy level 1      32 000 kJ
                    (fixed in carbohydrates by pond plants)

6400 kJ (released during respiration by pond plants)    ☐ (pond plants not consumed)

Energy level 2      20 480 kJ
                    (consumed by herbivores)

14 400 kJ (released during respiration)    468 kJ (herbivores not consumed)
                                            2046 kJ (contained in faeces)

Energy level 3      3566 kJ
                    (consumed by carnivores)

2300 kJ (released during respiration)    900 kJ (contained in faeces)

Use the information in the diagram and your own knowledge to answer the following questions.

(a) (i) By which process is the energy from sunlight fixed into carbohydrates? [1]
(ii) What percentage of the light energy which reached the pond was fixed into carbohydrates by the pond plants? Show your working. [2]
(iii) The remainder of the light energy which reached the pond was not fixed into carbohydrates by the pond plants. Suggest TWO reasons why this energy did not enter the food web. [2]
(b) Only 20 480 kJ per year reach the herbivores because the plants release energy from their carbohydrates during respiration and not all the plants are consumed. Work out the amount of energy still contained in the pond plants which were not consumed. Show your working. [2]
(c) Compare the amount of energy released during respiration by pond plants and by herbivores. Suggest ONE reason for the difference. [2]
(d) What may happen to the energy contained in the faeces produced by the herbivores? [2]
(e) Describe TWO ways in which energy from an aquatic food web may pass into a land-based food web. [4]

**Total 15 marks**
[ULEAC]

## Question 6

The diagram shows the mass of carbon involved each year in some of the processes in the carbon cycle.

(a) Complete the equation for plant respiration. [2]

☐ + oxygen → carbon dioxide + ☐ + energy

(b) (i) Calculate the mass of carbon removed from the atmosphere each year. Show your working. Answer .............................. billion tonnes [1]
(ii) Calculate the percentage of this total which is removed by the photosynthesis of land plants. Show your working. Answer .............................. % [2]
(c) Power stations often discharge warm water into rivers.
Describe how this warm water might affect organisms which live in the river. [3]
(d) The world-wide use of fossil fuels has increased rapidly during this century.
(i) Give **two** reasons for the increase in the amount of fossil fuels used. [2]
(ii) Give **two** effects on the environment of this increase in the amount of fossil fuels used. [2]
(iii) Describe and explain the long-term effects of large-scale deforestation on the Earth's atmosphere. [4]
(e) Give **two** reasons why the proportion of methane in the atmosphere is rising. [2]

[NEAB]

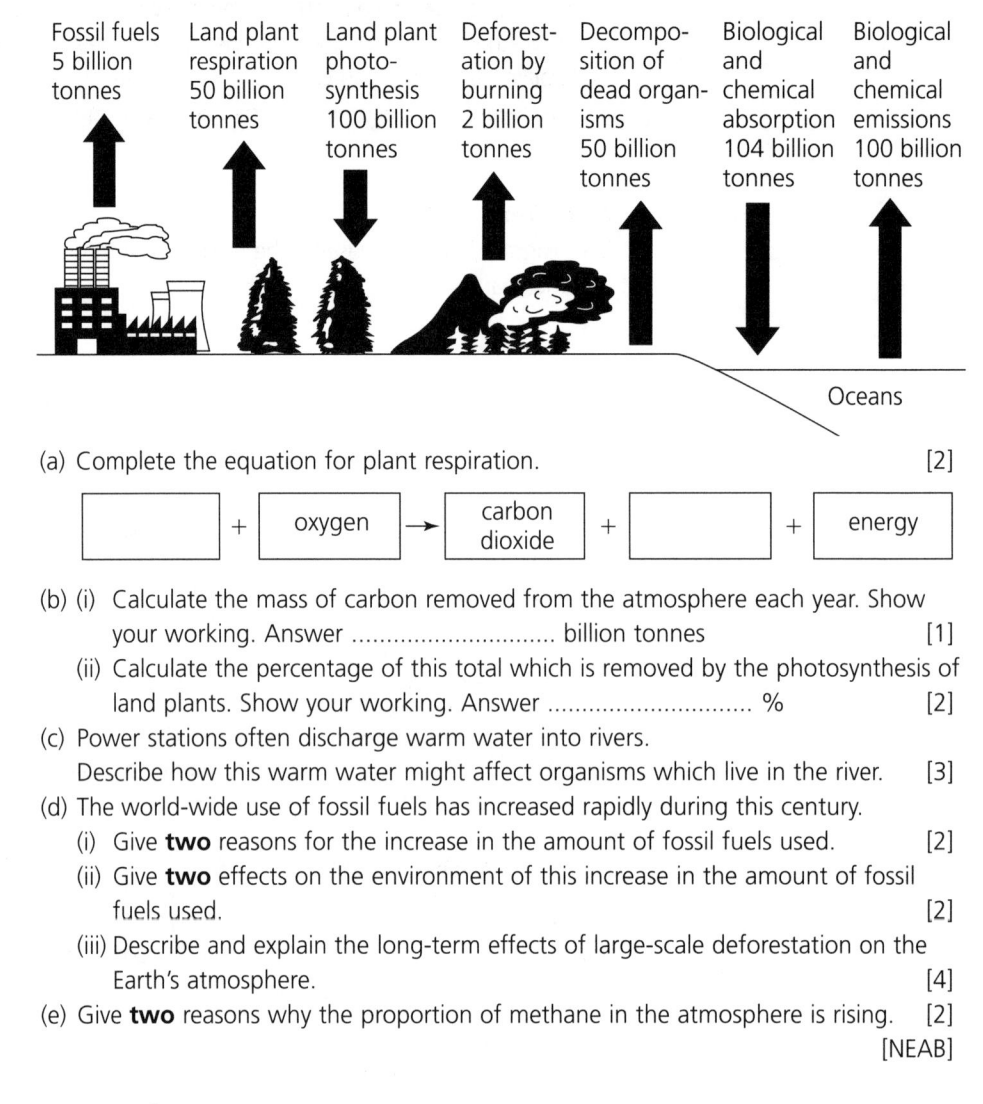

## Question 7

The diagram below shows the nitrogen cycle but some parts are missing.
(a) Complete the nitrogen cycle by writing the correct letter in each of the boxes provided. You may use each letter once, more than once or not at all. (table on p 51)

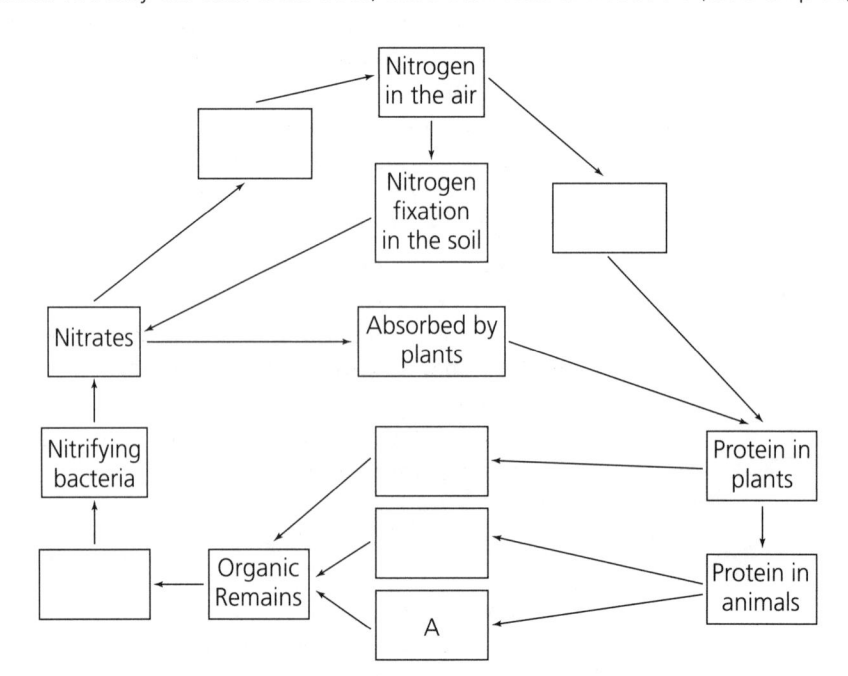

Choose the letters from the table below. The first one has been done for you. [5]

| Letter | A | B | C | D | E |
|---|---|---|---|---|---|
| **Part of nitrogen cycle** | Urine and faeces | Nitrogen fixation in root nodules e.g. of pea plants | Denitrifying bacteria | Death | Decay |

(b) Suggest what might happen to a plant if it could not absorb nitrates. [1]
(c) (i) Why is it important that nitrogen is cycled? [2]
   (ii) Carbon is also cycled. Name TWO processes which release carbon dioxide into the atmosphere. [2]

**Total 10 marks**
[ULEAC]

## Question 8

A farm is an ecosystem managed by a farmer. The crops grown at Green Mile Farm are barley, sugar beet and beans. Some organisms are pests which reduce the yield of the crop plants. Some pests, for example aphids, feed on crop plants and can pass viruses on to them. The farmer at Green Mile Farm wanted to make as much profit as possible. Table 1 below shows details of local pests. Table 2 shows agricultural chemicals which farmers can use.

**Table 1**

| Organism which reduces crop yield | How it over-winters | Crop affected | Effect |
|---|---|---|---|
| 'Take all' (fungus) | Lives on unploughed stubble and couch grass | Barley | Uses up plant's carbohydrates |
| Black bean aphid (insect) | Lives on weeds in hedgerows | Beans | Attacks the growing tips of bean plants |
| Couch grass (weed) | As seeds and underground stems | All crops | Competes with crops for resources |
| 'Yellows' (virus) | In stores of sugar beet and mangels | Sugar beet | Attacks leaf tissues which turn yellow |
| Beet aphid (insect) | Lives in beet stores and on weeds | Sugar beet | Penetrates tissues passing on viruses |

**Table 2**

| Agricultural chemical |
|---|
| Fertiliser |
| Insecticide |
| Fungicide |
| Herbicide |

Use the information above to answer the following questions.

(a) Which agricultural chemical would the farmer use to increase crop yield if there were no pests in the area? How would this help to achieve a greater yield? [2]
(b) Suggest THREE ways in which the farmer could prevent the fungus 'Take all' from harming his barley crop. [3]
(c) Table 1 states that couch grass competes with crops for resources.
   (i) How does competition lead to reduced crop yield? [2]
   (ii) What could the farmer use to get rid of the couch grass? [1]
(d) (i) When attached by the 'Yellows' virus, sugar beet leaves turn yellow. How will this reduce crop yield? [2]
   (ii) Viruses cannot move independently. How does the 'Yellows' virus enter the leaf tissues of the sugar beet? [2]
   (iii) How could the farmer prevent the 'Yellows' virus from attacking the sugar beet crop? [2]

(e) Suggest ONE environmental factor which should concern the farmer who uses agricultural chemicals. [1]

**Total 15 marks**
[ULEAC]

## Question 9
The diagram shows the design and operation of a system for farming prawns. The system is an example of a managed ecosystem.

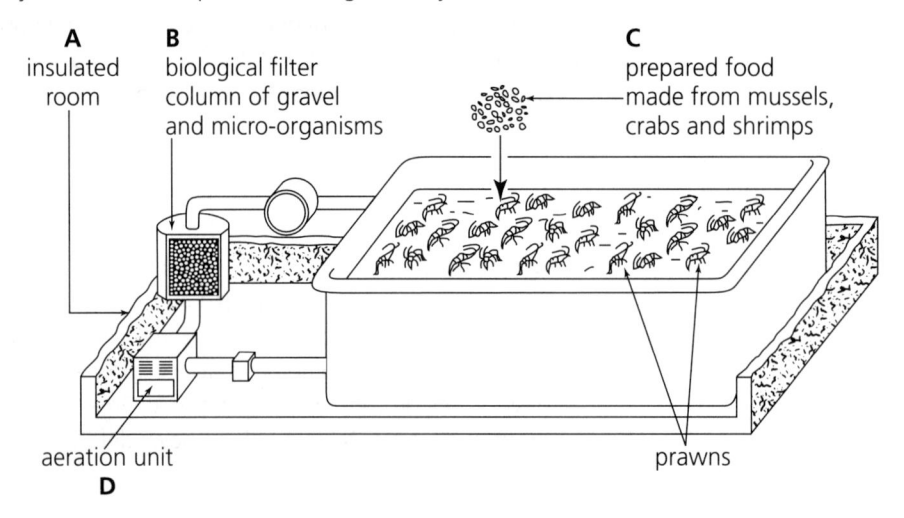

**A** insulated room

**B** biological filter column of gravel and micro-organisms

**C** prepared food made from mussels, crabs and shrimps

aeration unit
**D**

prawns

Explain why the factors **A**, **B**, **C** and **D** are carefully controlled in this managed ecosystem. [8]

[MEG]

# 6 Extension topics

Up to this point, all topics have been part of the National Curriculum for England and Wales at Key Stage 4, i.e. common with double award science. Each exam board can choose its own subject extension topics, which are studied in addition to the core topics for GCSE Biology. It is **vital** that you know which topics you must study: it will depend on which examination board syllabus you are following.

## REVISION TIPS

The extension topics are usually tested in a separate written paper lasting one to one and a half hours; they account for 25 per cent of your final mark. That means that this area of your syllabus will be tested very thoroughly and you should spend extra time revising this work. Make sure that you can label key diagrams and that you understand the main stages in manufacturing processes, e.g. of foods, enzymes, antibiotics, etc.

Some of the extension topics overlap with information in the subject core, e.g. immunity, genetic engineering, so try to link related areas when you are revising.

Find out if your examination board sets a completely separate extension paper, or whether it will include some core topics, and target your revision accordingly.

## TOPIC OUTLINE

Since each examination board chooses its own extension topics, it is impossible to cover all the possible points in this book. However, there is a considerable amount of overlap between examination boards and this is a summary of some of the most common topics.

### Micro-organisms

- There are **four** main types of **micro-organisms**: bacteria, viruses, fungi and protoctists (protozoa).
- Micro-organisms may be helpful to humans, e.g. used in food production, harmful to humans, e.g. cause diseases in humans (or in animals or plants humans depend on), or may have little effect on humans.
  Micro-organisms which cause **disease** are known as **pathogens**.
  Micro-organisms (or other living things) which live in or on a living organism and cause it harm are known as **parasites**.
- **Bacteria** are single-celled organisms about 1/1000 mm in diameter. Their shape varies according to their type, e.g. spherical, rod-shaped, helical. They have a single chromosome made of DNA but no proper nucleus, and their cytoplasm is surrounded by a cell wall. They reproduce by **binary fission** (a simple form of asexual reproduction).
  Some bacteria are pathogens, e.g. causing salmonella, cholera, TB.
  Some bacteria are useful, e.g. in manufacture of yoghurt, cheese, vinegar.
  Many bacteria have little effect on humans.

- **Viruses** are much smaller than bacteria and can only multiply inside the cells of a living organism. They have a very simple structure: a small piece of nucleic acid (RNA or DNA) surrounded by a protein coat (the capsid) and possibly an outer envelope. Viruses do not have a nucleus or cytoplasm and they do not carry out the basic life processes, e.g. feeding, respiration, excretion, etc.
  They replicate (copy themselves) inside a host cell, and usually kill the host cell when they are released.
  All viruses are parasites and all viruses are pathogenic to their host. Some viruses cause disease in humans, e.g. measles, flu, AIDS, hepatitis.
- **Fungi** are bigger than bacteria and may be single celled, e.g. yeasts, or multi-cellular, e.g. moulds, mushrooms. Fungi have a proper nucleus and cytoplasm and cells are surrounded by a cell wall. **Multi-cellular** fungi consist of a mycelium made up of branched hyphae and reproduce by releasing **spores**. **Unicellular fungi** are spherical or oval and reproduce by **budding** (simple asexual reproduction) or by **sexual reproduction**.
  Some fungi are pathogens, e.g. causing athlete's foot, and many plant diseases. Some fungi are useful, e.g. in baking and brewing, in the manufacture of antibiotics, as a food source.
  Many fungi have little effect on humans.
- **Protoctists** (protozoa) are single-celled, simple organisms. Some are similar to plants (algae) and are very important as producers in food chains. Others are similar to animal cells, e.g. amoeba, and feed on organic material. They have a nucleus and cytoplasm, and some have a cellulose cell wall.
  Some protoctists are pathogens, e.g. causing malaria and a type of dysentery. Some protoctists are useful, e.g. as a food source for humans or animals. Most protoctists have little effect on humans.
- Bacteria and fungi can be grown in the lab on petri dishes containing nutrient agar, or in vessels called fermenters. The culture medium must contain carbohydrate and minerals, and some microbes need vitamins or proteins in addition to this. Conditions for growth must be carefully controlled, e.g. optimum temperature, pH and air supply, to get maximum yield.
- Viruses can only survive inside living cells, so they are difficult to grow in the laboratory.
- Protoctists can be grown in fermenters: some will need light in order to photosynthesise.
- Aseptic technique is very important when handling microbes. This prevents contamination of the microbes you are growing with other organisms, and prevents contamination of the laboratory environment.

### Micro-organisms and disease

- Not all diseases are caused by microbes: some are **genetic**, e.g. cystic fibrosis, some are **environmental**, e.g. lung cancer, some are **degenerative**, e.g. arthritis, some are **dietary**, e.g. scurvy.
- Pathogenic bacteria can enter the body in food and water, they can be breathed in, or transferred by direct contact.
- **Antibiotics** damage bacterial cells walls and will kill bacteria. They are ineffective against viruses, fungi or protoctists.
- Some bacterial infections can be avoided by careful food handling and storage, and by good personal hygiene. Proper cooking will kill bacteria in food and disinfectants will kill bacteria in the home environment.
- Pathogenic viruses can enter the body in food or water but they are usually breathed in, or transferred by direct contact. They will invade cells and replicate inside them, causing tissue damage when they are released.

- Viruses can only be treated with anti-viral drugs and some of these have serious side effects. Many viral infections can be avoided by **immunisation** (vaccination).
- Pathogenic fungi are normally transferred by direct contact. Infections can be treated with anti-fungal drugs.
- Pathogenic protoctists may enter the body through contaminated food or water, or may be spread by an animal vector, e.g. malaria is spread by mosquitoes.
- The human body has several defence mechanisms to combat pathogens including:
  (a) phagocytic white blood cells which engulf pathogens;
  (b) antibodies made by lymphocytes.
  These mechanisms are called **natural immunity**. Immunisation (vaccination) can improve the body's response to infection. This is called **acquired immunity**.

## Biotechnology

This is the use of micro-organisms to make products useful to humans, or to carry out complex processes. Examples of biotechnology include food production, sewage treatment, production of enzymes, fuels and pharmaceutical products, e.g. antibiotics, hormones, vitamins and vaccines.

- **Yeasts** (fungi) respire anaerobically if they are grown without oxygen.

  glucose → energy + carbon dioxide + ethanol

  This reaction (sometimes called **fermentation**) is very important for brewing and baking.
- Many fungi will produce **antibiotics**, e.g. penicillin: these are chemicals which slow the growth of bacteria, or even kill them. If fungi are grown in fermenters, in the right conditions, large amounts of antibiotics can be obtained.
- Some fungi can be used to make human or animal foods (**mycoprotein**), e.g. moulds grown in a fermenter are processed to make 'Quorn'. This is high in protein and fibre and low in cholesterol and fat.
- Some bacteria (called lactic acid bacteria) can convert **lactose** (a type of sugar found in milk) into **lactic acid**. This is the basis of yoghurt production and is also important in the manufacture of cheese.
- Some bacteria convert **alcohol** into **vinegar** when there is oxygen present. These are called acetic acid bacteria.
- Many bacteria and fungi are used to manufacture **enzymes**. The enzymes can be used in biological washing powders, in food processing, e.g. as flour improvers, as meat tenderisers, in confectionery production, in baby foods (to 'pre-digest' food) and in brewing.
- Some bacteria can be used to convert **plant waste**, e.g. sugar cane waste, into **ethanol** for use as a fuel. This is known as **gasohol** and can be mixed with petrol for use in cars.
- Some bacteria can be used to convert **domestic waste**, e.g. human and animal faeces, biodegradable rubbish, into **methane gas** for use as fuel. This is know as **biogas** and can be used for heating, to work machinery, etc.
- Some bacteria and fungi are very important in **sewage treatment**. They are decomposers, and they break down organic material in urine and faeces to form carbon dioxide and water.
- Bacteria and fungi can be changed by **genetic engineering** to produce human hormones, e.g. insulin, growth hormones, or to make vaccines.
- Domestic plants and animals can be changed by genetic engineering to produce products containing vaccines,

e.g. milk which provides immunity from diseases;
potatoes/bananas which provide immunity from disease.

## Movement and support

Animals have a **skeleton** which helps to support the body and is used in movement. In **vertebrates** this is an **internal skeleton**, made of bone or cartilage. In **invertebrates** the skeleton may be an **external covering**, e.g. in insects, crustaceans, or may be a **core of fluid**, e.g. hydrostatic skeleton of earthworms.

▶ **Bones** are made of minerals and protein and contain living bone cells. They are strong and resist compression. They act as **levers** when they are moved by **muscles**. **Cartilage** covers the joint surfaces to reduce friction. **Ligaments** stabilise joints.

▶ **Muscles** can contract to move bones. They are attached to bones by **tendons** (these cannot change in length), so when muscles contract, bones are pulled closer together. Muscles always work in **pairs** (antagonistic pairs), e.g. biceps and triceps, which have opposite effects.

▶ **Animals** are adapted for locomotion in a particular habitat. Many vertebrates have a **pentadactyl** limb pattern, but the detailed structure depends on the function of the limb,
e.g. in birds, forelimbs are adapted as wings for flight;
in the mole, forelimbs are adapted as strong legs for digging.

▶ **Birds** have strong, light bones to reduce body mass for flight. **Wings** provide an aerofoil shape and **feathers** provide a very large surface area with minimum mass. Birds have large breast muscles to move the wings for flapping flight.

▶ **Fish** are a streamlined shape and have **scales** that reduce friction to allow efficient movement. **Paired fins** reduce pitching, and allow the animal to change direction. **Median fins** reduce yawing and rolling (side to side movement). Muscle blocks arranged in a zig-zag pattern around the vertebral column produce a wave-like movement along the length of the body, and many fish have a **swim bladder** for buoyancy.

▶ Some **protoctists** can move through water by beating **cilia** or **flagella**, or can change shape to creep across the substrate.

▶ Plant movements are called **tropisms** – a tropism is a growth movement in response to a stimulus,
e.g. shoots grow towards light (this is phototropism);
roots grow downwards (stimulus is gravity: this is geotropism).
Tropisms depend on the production of **hormones**, e.g. auxin, by the root or shoot tip.

## REVISION ACTIVITY

**1** (a) Label this diagram of a bacterium.

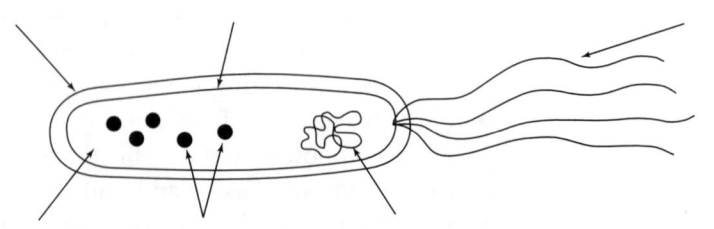

(b) Give three ways it is different to a virus.
(c) Place these micro-organisms into size order (smallest first)
yeast      virus      bacterium      mould

## extension topics

**2** Look at this diagram of a fermenter.

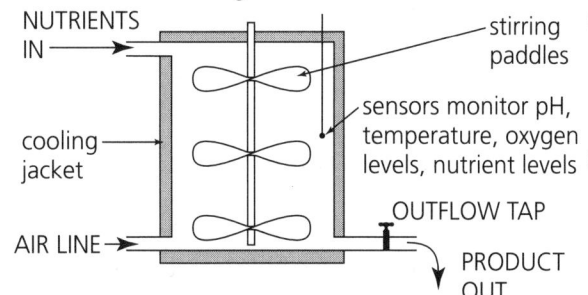

NUTRIENTS IN → stirring paddles
sensors monitor pH, temperature, oxygen levels, nutrient levels
cooling jacket
AIR LINE →
OUTFLOW TAP
PRODUCT OUT

(a) Explain the purpose of
 (i) the cooling jacket
 (ii) the stirrer
 (iii) the air line
(b) suggest an optimum temperature for the growth of bacteria. Give a reason for your choice.

**3** Match up each of the types of micro-organism with two words or phrases from the box (not all words in the box are used).

(a) bacteria  ........  ........
(b) yeast  ........  ........
(c) viruses  ........  ........
(d) moulds  ........  ........

| replication | photosynthesis | capsid |
| hyphae | binary fission | budding |
| brewing | malaria | amoeba |
| vinegar | mycoprotein | algae |

**4** Careful food handling and storage will prevent many cases of food poisoning. Give a reason for each of the following kitchen rules.
(a) Store raw meat in the fridge until it is ready to be cooked.
(b) Make sure frozen food is properly defrosted before cooking.
(c) Store raw meat at the bottom of the fridge, not the top.
(d) Keep separate chopping boards and knives for meat and bread.
(e) Boil dishcloths regularly, or replace disposable dishcloths.

**5** Give three reasons why it is useful to produce gasohol from plant waste.

**6** (a) Put these diagrams of stages of genetic engineering into the correct order:

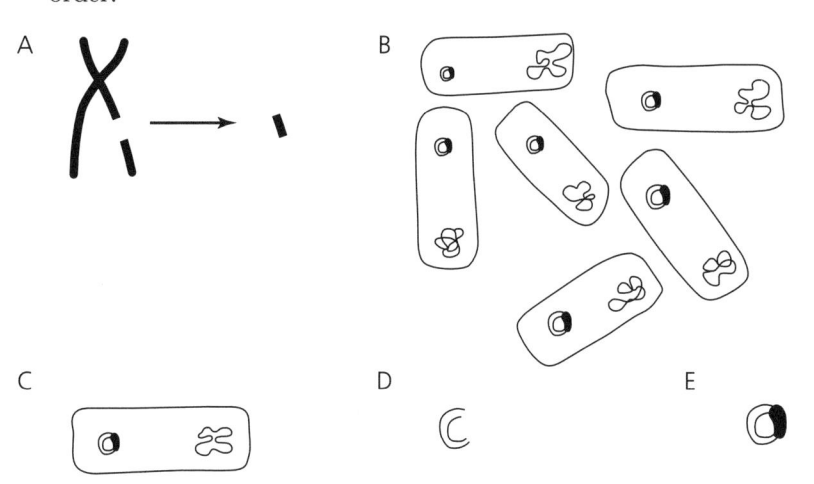

A   B   C   D   E

Correct order: _____
(b) Explain how this process is used in the manufacture of vegetarian cheese.

**7** (a) Label this diagram showing how the arm moves.

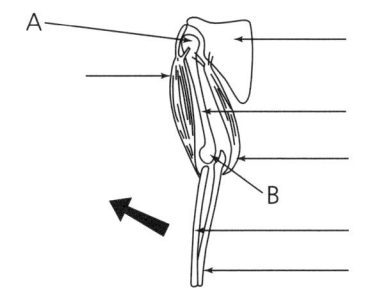

(b) Explain why tendons are inelastic.
(c) What type of joint is found at:
 A? ..........................
 B? ..........................

**8** (a) Define a tropism.
(b) Shoots are **negatively geotropic**. Explain what this term means.

(c) Three shoots were treated as shown and illuminated from one side. Which set of alternatives correctly shows what would happen after one week?

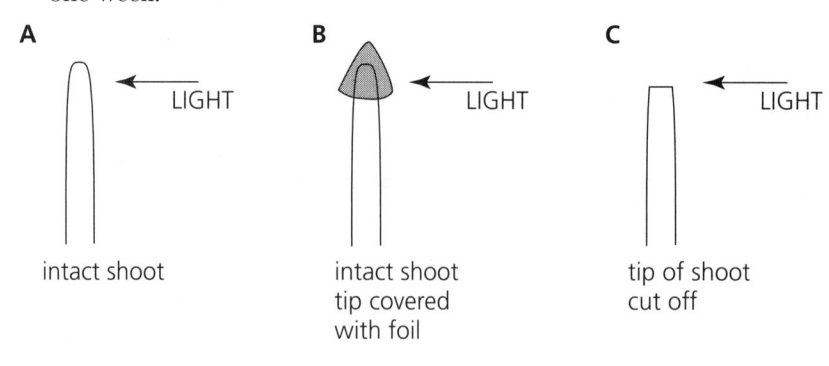

|   | Shoot A | Shoot B | Shoot C |
|---|---------|---------|---------|
| 1 | bends to left | bends to right | does not bend |
| 2 | bends to right | bends to right | bends to right |
| 3 | does not bend | does not bend | does not bend |
| 4 | bends to right | bends to left | does not bend |
| 5 | bends to right | does not bend | does not bend |

Correct answer = .......... Explain why this occurs.

# EXAMINATION QUESTIONS

### Question 1
(a) Look carefully at diagrams A, B and C below and state which is a virus, a bacterium and yeast. [3]

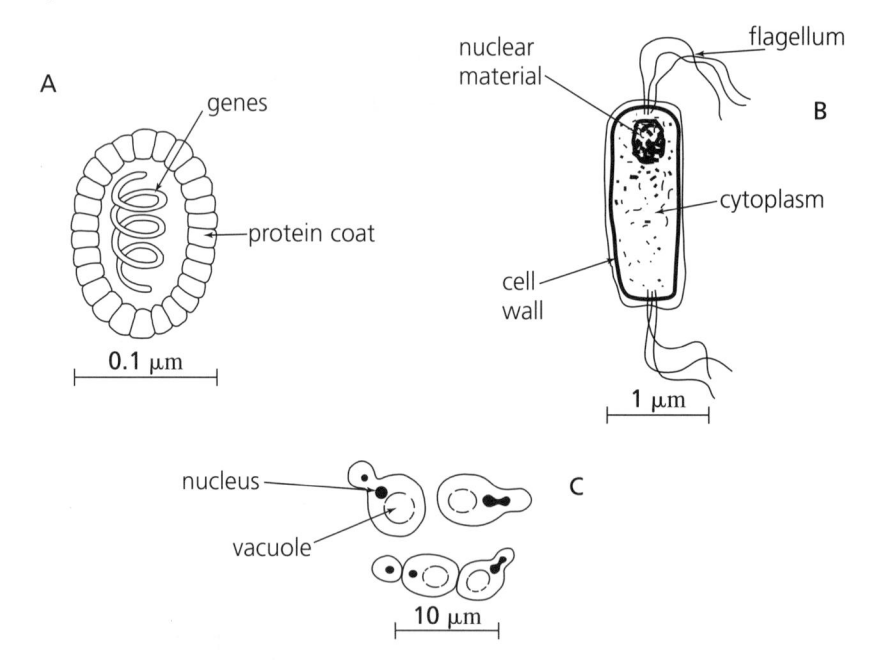

Underline the correct answer in each of the following statements.
(b) Viruses are
   (i) smaller than bacteria   (ii) bigger than bacteria   (iii) the same size as bacteria
(c) Yeast is
   (i) a fungus   (ii) an alga   (iii) a virus
(d) A virus can be grown in a laboratory in
   (i) hens' eggs   (ii) sugar solutions   (iii) water   [3]

[WJEC]

### Question 2

The graphs shows the rate of growth of a fungus and the production of an antibiotic in a fermenter.

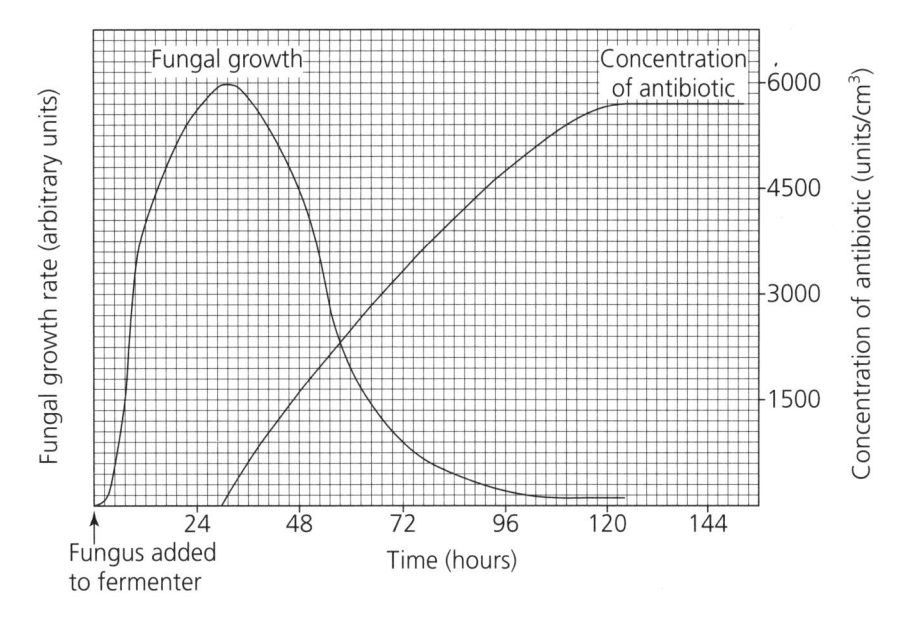

(a) When would be the best time to stop the fermentation process and harvest the antibiotic?
    Give a reason for your answer. [2]
(b) Give TWO ways in which the **rate** of antibiotic production could have been increased. [2]
(c) Some streptococci cause infectious diseases which can be controlled by the use of antibiotics.
    (i) What are streptococci? [1]
    (ii) How can streptococci be transmitted from one person to another? [1]
(d) In 1950, a dose of a few units of an antibiotic was enough to cure a streptococcal infection. In 1990, a much larger dose of the same antibiotic was needed to cure the same streptococcal infection.
    Give and explain ONE reason for the change in the amount of antibiotic needed to treat a streptococcal infection. [1]
(e) Many doctors are concerned that, in the future, antibiotics may not cure streptococcal infections at all. Suggest ONE reason for their concern. [1]
(f) Suggest TWO ways in which the number of cases of streptococcal infections could be reduced in the future even if antibiotics failed to cure them. [2]

**Total 10 marks**
[ULEAC]

### Question 3

Micro-organisms are involved in the production of several types of food.

(a) During the manufacture of cheese, milk proteins form a solid material (curd) from which the liquid whey is drained. Micro-organisms ferment lactose sugar in the milk, resulting in a lowering of the pH. The enzyme rennin may then be added in the form of rennet which is a natural extract from the dried stomach of calves.
    (i) What type of micro-organisms are used to ferment lactose sugar? [1]
    (ii) How is the lowering of the pH actually achieved? [1]
    (iii) What directly results from the lowering of the pH? [1]
(b) During recent years the enzyme rennin (chymosin) has been manufactured from genetically engineered bacteria. This has involved the identification of genes for the production of rennin and the cloning of these genes in E coli bacteria. The enzyme produced from these bacteria is often used as a substitute for rennet in the manufacture of some types of cheese.

(i) Describe briefly how genetic engineering and cloning can be used to produce rennin (chymosin) from bacteria. [5]
(ii) What objections do some people have to genetically engineered food? [2]
(iii) What are the benefits of producing rennin (chymosin) using genetically engineered micro-organisms? [3]

(c) Modern methods of making vinegar are among the few methods, using micro-organisms, which run on a continuous culture system. Fig. 1 is a simplified diagram of one method of vinegar production.

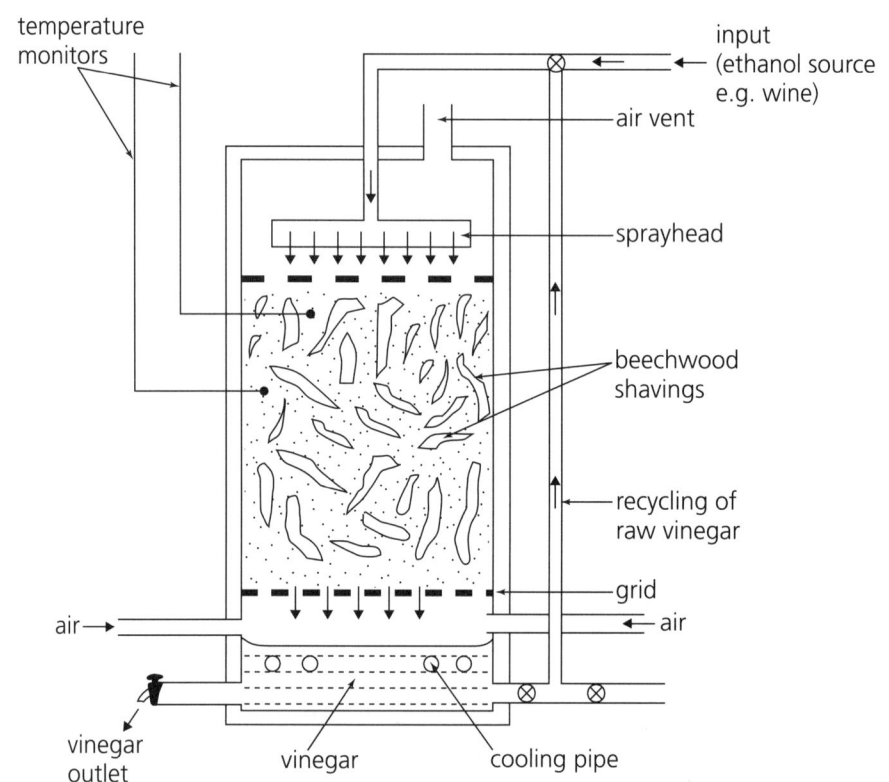

*Fig. 1*

(i) Name the type of micro-organism which forms a film over the wood shavings. [1]
(ii) What is meant by 'continuous culture system'? [2]
(iii) Why is it essential that air is supplied during the process and how do the wood shavings help in this respect? [3]
(iv) What main chemical change is brought about by the micro-organisms during the process? [1]
(v) Why must the temperature be carefully monitored? [2]

[MEG]

### Question 4

(a) People can suffer from these diseases: athlete's foot, scurvy, common cold, tetanus and whooping cough.
Which of these diseases
(i) is not infectious?
(ii) is caused by a virus?
(iii) is caused by a fungus? [3]

(b) State TWO differences between an antiseptic and an antibiotic. [2]

(c) A student cut three discs of filter paper and labelled them A, B and C. Disc A was soaked in distilled water, B in a low concentration of an antibiotic solution and C in a higher concentration of the antibiotic solution. The three discs were placed on to a petri dish containing bacteria. Fig. 2 shows the results after 24 hours.

### extension topics

*Fig. 2*

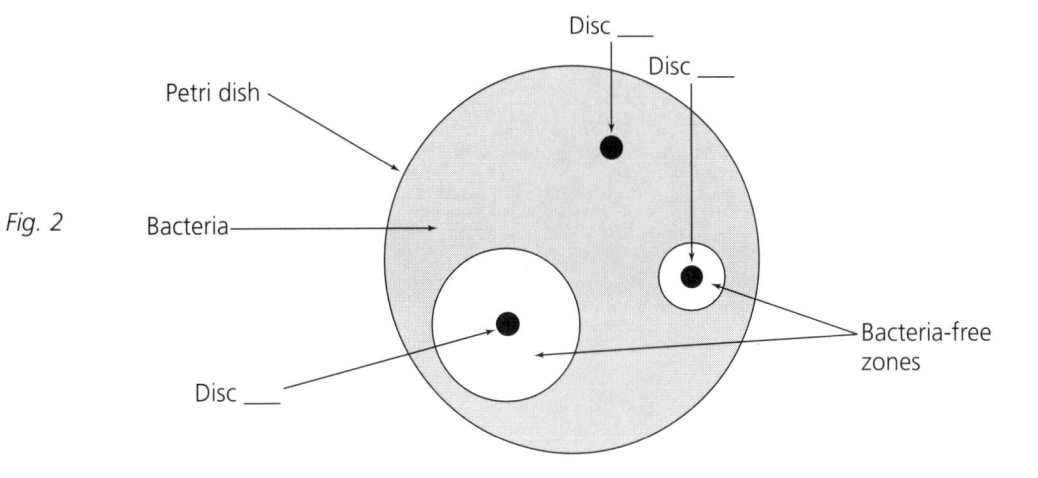

Labels on diagram: Disc __, Disc __, Petri dish, Bacteria, Bacteria-free zones, Disc __

(i) Label Fig. 2 to show which disc was which. [3]
(ii) Explain the choices you made in (c) (i). [4]
(iii) Suggest why the student included Disc A in the experiment. [1]

[MEG]

**Question 5**

(a) Micro-organisms are often described as parasites or pathogens.
  (i) What does the term parasite mean? [2]
  (ii) What does the term pathogen mean? [1]
(b) What effect do antibiotics have on infectious bacteria and viruses?
  bacteria .................... viruses .................... [2]
(c) Using **ONLY** the information in the following paragraph answer (i) to (iv).

  There are two main forms of immunity, natural and acquired. Acquired immunity may be of two types, namely passive and active.
  Passive immunity is obtained by injecting the serum of an animal which has previously had a mild infection of the disease. The animal's own immune system will have produced antibodies for that disease. The antibodies retain their effectiveness when injected into humans.
  Active acquired immunity involves the body making its own antibodies over a long period of time.
  There are three methods of acquiring immunity actively:
  by inoculating with a vaccine containing a weakened micro-organism e.g. smallpox; by inoculating with a vaccine containing dead micro-organisms e.g. whooping cough; and by inoculating with modified toxins produced by harmful micro-organisms.

  (i) What is the source of antibodies in each of the two types of acquired immunity?
    passive .................... active .................... [2]
  (ii) Of the two forms of acquired immunity which does a human acquire quicker? [1]
  (iii) Under what circumstances would it be extremely beneficial to use the passive method of acquiring immunity? [1]
  (iv) Suggest why weakened or dead micro-organisms are used rather than live micro-organisms in the vaccines used to promote active immunity. [2]

(d) Malaria is a disease which affects human beings. The organism which causes the disease lives in the bloodstream of the infected person.
  (i) Name the organism which causes malaria. [1]
  (ii) Describe briefly how this organism is transferred from one human to another and so causes the disease to spread. [4]
  (iii) State **THREE** steps which can be taken to reduce the likelihood of transfer. [3]

[MEG]

# part III
# Answers and grading

# Solutions
## Life processes and cell activity

### SOLUTION TO REVISION ACTIVITY

1 Cell membrane, chloroplast, nucleus, cytoplasm.
2 Cell A = red blood cell.  Function = carrying oxygen.
   Adaptations – contains haemoglobin to carry oxygen
   – has a large surface area due to biconcave disc shape
   – has no nucleus so it can contain more oxygen
   Cell B = nerve cell (neurone).  Function = transmitting nerve impulses.
   Adaptations – has a long axon to connect it to other structures
   – has many dendrites so it can form a nerve network
   – has a myelin sheath to speed up transmission of impulses

3

| Plant cells | Animal cells |
| --- | --- |
| have a cellulose cell wall | do not have a cellulose cell wall |
| have a large sap vacuole | do not have a large sap vacuole |
| may contain chloroplasts | never contain chloroplasts |

   **NB** do **not** give shape as a difference – the shape varies between cell types, e.g. palisade cells and guard cells are completely different to each other.

4 Osmosis is the movement of **water** from an area of **high** concentration of water, to an area of **lower** concentration of water, through a **semi-permeable membrane**.
5 The liquid level would fall, because water is moving out of the thistle funnel by osmosis.  The concentration of water molecules is higher in the funnel (pure water) than in the beaker (salt solution).
6 The potato pieces got bigger because water moved into them by osmosis.  Solution X is pure water, or a very weak solution of sugar or salt.
7 C B D A E
8

| Mitosis | Meiosis |
| --- | --- |
| produces two daughter cells | produces four daughter cells |
| number of chromosomes equal to number in original cell | number of chromosomes is halved |
| daughter cells identical to original cell | daughter cells not identical to original cell |
| occurs in growth and repair | occurs in gamete formation |

### ANSWERS TO EXAMINATION QUESTIONS

*Question 1*

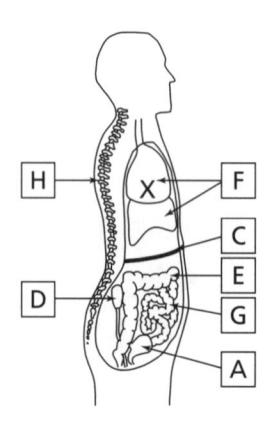

### Question 2
D, G, C, F, E, A, B, H, A

### Question 3

*Examiner's note* This question tests your understanding of osmosis. The balance allows you to work out whether water is moving into or out of the potato/Visking tubing bag.

(a) The balance is higher on the left hand side because water is moving out of the potato/Visking tubing bag [1] by osmosis. Osmosis is the movement of water from an area of high concentration of water molecules, e.g. distilled water [1], to an area of lower concentration of water molecules, e.g. concentrated sugar solution [1].
The balance is lower on the right hand side because water is moving into the potato/Visking tubing bag by osmosis [1].

(b) Concentration of sap = 10 per cent
Reason: the angle of the balance beam indicates how much water has moved. In the last experiment the angle is 15.5 degrees, and the Visking tubing bag contains a 10 per cent sugar solution. In the first experiment the angle is 15.5 degrees, so the *Cara* potato cell sap must be a 10 per cent solution.

## 2 Humans as organisms

### SOLUTION TO REVISION ACTIVITY

1

| Food group | Food containing it | Functions in the body |
|---|---|---|
| Carbohydrate | **sugary foods, starchy foods** | **provides energy** |
| **Lipid** | butter, cheese, red meat, fried foods | **provides energy** |
| **Protein** | **meat, fish, cheese, eggs** | growth and repair, making enzymes |
| **Fibre** | **vegetables, fruit** | keeps the digestive system healthy, prevents constipation |
| **Minerals** | meat, milk, green vegetables | **prevent anaemia and brittle bones** |
| **Vitamins** | **green vegetables, fruits** | prevent scurvy and rickets. Needed for healthy skin and bones |

2

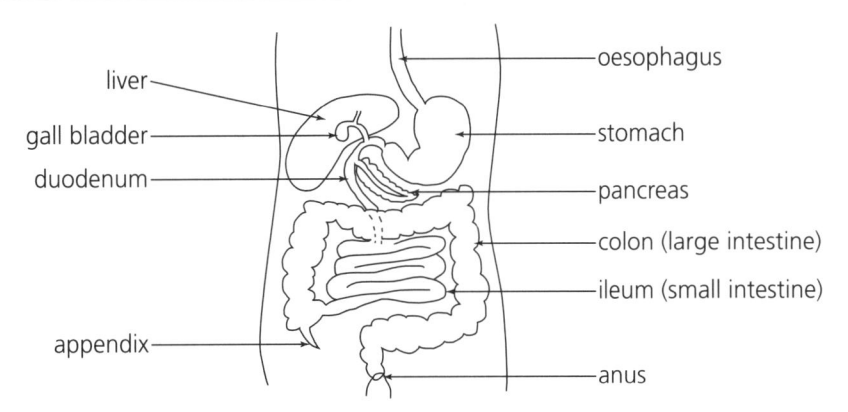

Labels: liver, gall bladder, duodenum, appendix, oesophagus, stomach, pancreas, colon (large intestine), ileum (small intestine), anus

3 Enzymes are catalysts made by the body. They control the rate of chemical reactions, e.g. digestion.
Graph A shows the effect of temperature.
Graph B shows the effect of pH.

**4**

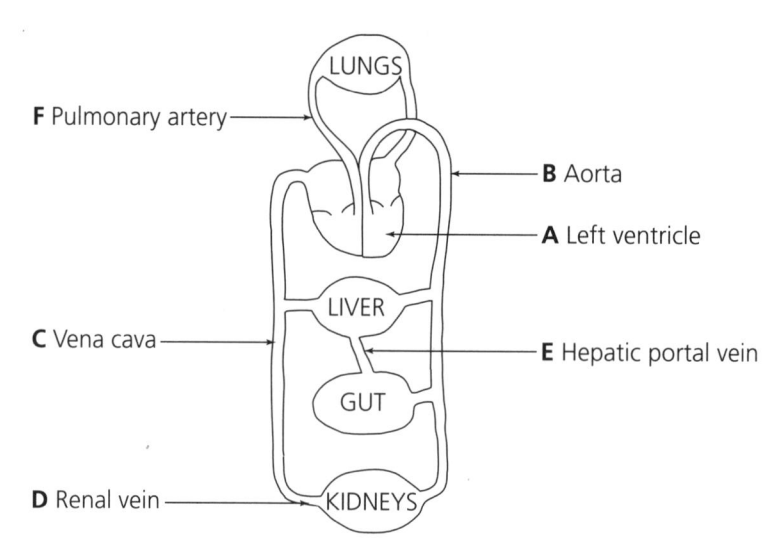

- **F** Pulmonary artery
- **B** Aorta
- **A** Left ventricle
- **C** Vena cava
- **E** Hepatic portal vein
- **D** Renal vein

The pulmonary artery carries deoxygenated blood.

**5** When a person breathes in, the diaphragm (<u>contracts</u>/relaxes) so it becomes more (<u>flat</u>/dome shaped). The external intercostal muscles (<u>contract</u>/relax) so the rib cage moves (down and in/<u>up and out</u>). The volume of the thorax (decreases/<u>increases</u>) so the pressure in the thorax (<u>decreases</u>/increases) and air moves (<u>in</u>/out).

**6**

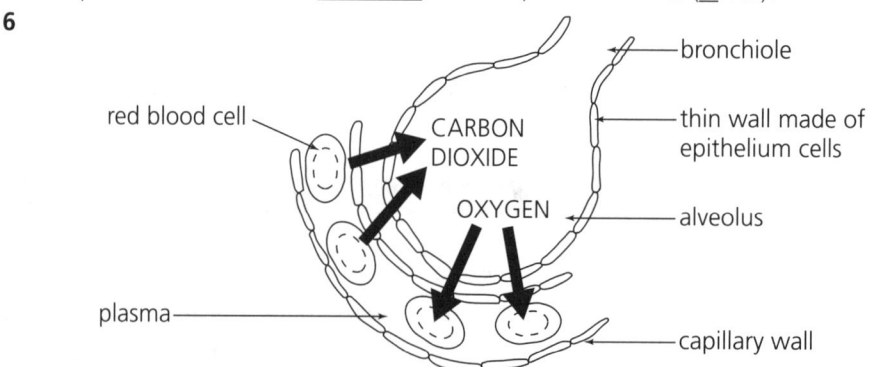

The alveolus is adapted for gas exchange because it:
(a) has a thin wall (one cell thick)
(b) is moist
(c) is permeable
(d) provides a large surface area for exchange to occur
(e) has a good blood supply

**7** glucose + oxygen → energy + carbon dioxide + water.

**8**

| Factor | Increases/Decreases/Stays the same | Reason |
| --- | --- | --- |
| Heart rate | Increases | to deliver more food and oxygen to muscles |
| Breathing rate | Increases | to get more oxygen into the body |
| Lactic acid | Increases | because anaerobic respiration is occurring |
| Glycogen in liver/muscle | Decreases | it is being changed to glucose and used |
| Body temperature | Increases | respiration makes heat |

**9 B E C A D**

# answers and grading

10 Light enters the eye through a hole called the **pupil**. This changes in diameter when muscles in the **iris** contract, so the amount of light entering the eye varies. The light is focused on to the **retina** by the **lens.** This changes shape when the **ciliary** muscle contracts or relaxes. To look at a distant object, the lens must be **long** and **thin**, so the ciliary muscle is **relaxed**. The retina contains two types of light-sensitive cells, called **rods** and **cones**; the **cones** are most common near to the **yellow** spot, and they are capable of detecting **colour**.

11 (a) 28 days
   (b) (i) day 14   (ii) 1–6   (iii) 11–18
   (c) oestrogen and progesterone
   (d) progesterone

12

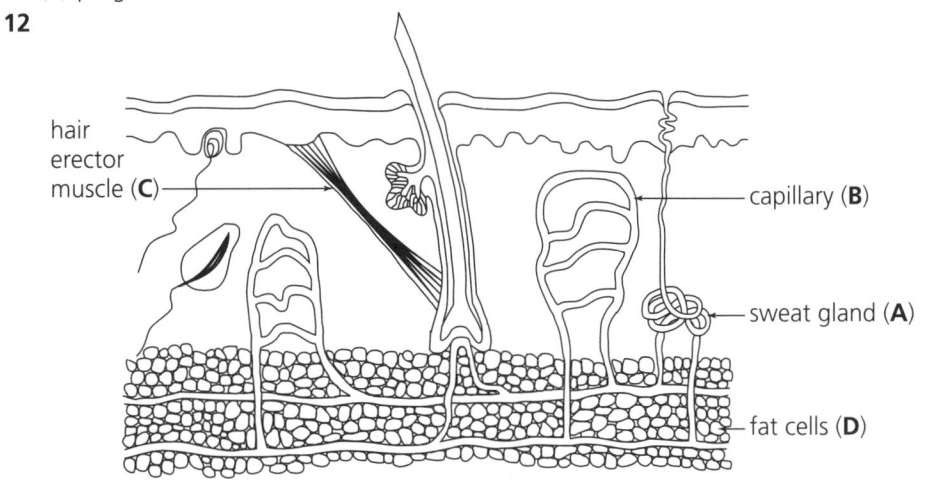

(labels: hair erector muscle (C); capillary (B); sweat gland (A); fat cells (D))

14 Homeostasis means that conditions inside the body remain constant at the optimum (correct) level.

| Hormone | Gland making it | Target organ | Effect |
| --- | --- | --- | --- |
| Insulin | pancreas | liver and muscle | glucose is absorbed from blood and stored as glycogen |
| ADH | pituitary | kidney tubule | more water is reabsorbed, therefore less urine produced |
| Adrenaline | adrenal | heart, lungs, muscles, blood vessels | prepares the body to respond to danger |

## ANSWERS TO EXAMINATION QUESTIONS

### Question 1
(a)

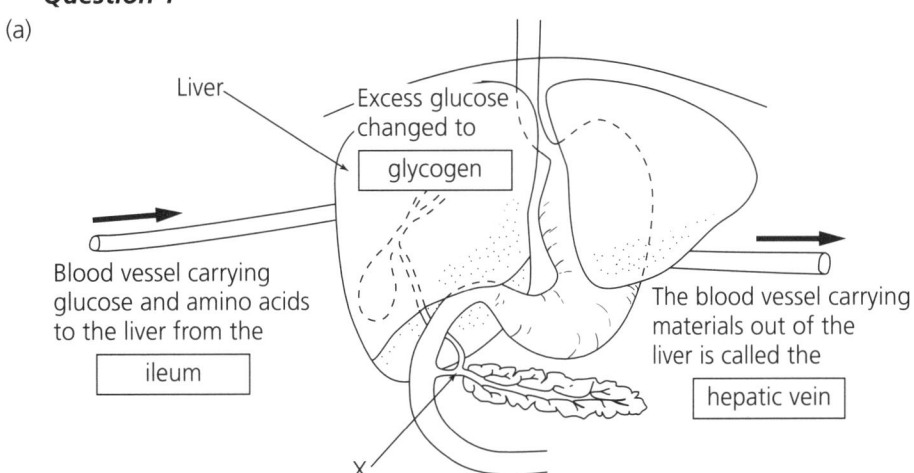

(labels: Liver; Excess glucose changed to glycogen; Blood vessel carrying glucose and amino acids to the liver from the ileum; The blood vessel carrying materials out of the liver is called the hepatic vein; X)

(b)

| Class of food | Chemical elements present |
| --- | --- |
| Carbohydrate | carbon, hydrogen, oxygen |
| Protein | carbon, hydrogen, oxygen, nitrogen |
| Fat | carbon, hydrogen, oxygen |

(c) Digestive enzymes are essential because they **can help break down large molecules**.

(d) Graph D – enzymes work slowly at low temperature and are denatured at high temperatures. The optimum temperature is 37°C.

### Question 2

(a) Smoking cigarettes increases the risk of bronchitis – the more you smoke, the more likely you are to have the disease.

(b) (i) Mucus stops moving because cilia no longer beat to move mucus towards the head.

(ii) Mucus accumulates in alveoli and bronchioles [1]. It irritates the air passages and they may become infected [1]. Coughing is a reflex action to remove mucus [1].

(iii) When alveoli are clogged with mucus, gas exchange is less efficient, so less oxygen enters the body.
Smokers may suffer from emphysema, where walls of the alveoli break down and the surface area for gas exchange is decreased.

(c) (i) Bronchitis is an infection of the bronchi and bronchioles, causing large amounts of mucus to be produced. This can partially block the airways, making breathing and gas exchange difficult and reducing the amount of oxygen entering the blood.

(ii) Antibiotics became available to fight infection.
Air pollution decreased (so lung diseases like bronchitis were less likely to be fatal).

(iii) More women were smoking cigarettes.
Women were smoking larger numbers of cigarettes.

(d) (i) In all body cells

(ii) To make energy

### Question 3

(a) C = blind spot        E = iris
    D = optic nerve      F = cornea

(b) **A** lens – focuses light on to the retina.
**B** retina – contains light-sensitive cells to detect light/convert light energy into a nerve impulse.

(c) (i) 6 whiskies

(ii) Distance fallen in last test = 72 cm
Distance fallen in first test = 8 cm
The ruler fell 72/8 = **9** times further in the last test

### Question 4

(a) (i) An increase in hormone Y causes
1 the uterus lining to become thicker
2 the ovum to be released from the ovary

(ii) Oestrogen

(b) (i) Menstruation/period

(ii) A **fall** in the level of **progesterone** causes menstruation.

(c) (i) If the level of progesterone stays high:
the uterus lining stays thick, i.e. the woman does not have a period;
the next follicle does not develop in the ovary/ovulation will not occur.

(ii) Any two of:
she is taking the contraceptive pill;
she is pregnant;
the placenta is making progesterone (if she is pregnant);
the corpus luteum is making progesterone (if she is pregnant).
(d) (i) Low progesterone stimulates (causes) ovulation [1].
Reason: Luteinising hormone is needed to make ovulation occur.
High progesterone levels stop production of luteinising hormone/low progesterone levels increase production of luteinising hormone.
(ii) Negative feedback.

**Examiner's note** You are not expected to *know* the information in the flow chart for part (d), but you should be able to *use* the information you are given to answer the question.

## Question 5
(a) Excretion is removal of waste products [1] made inside the body [1].
(b) (i) A = kidney cortex    B= medulla    C = ureter
(ii) urine    (iii) bladder
(iv) Vena cava

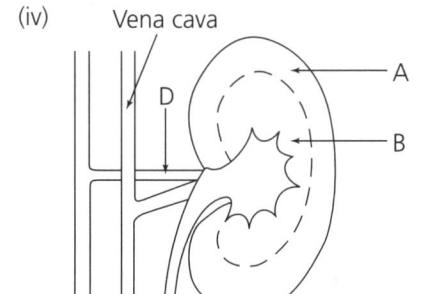

(c) (i) Protein or glucose
Protein: protein molecules are too big to pass out of the capillary into the nephron by ultrafiltration.
Glucose: glucose molecules pass from the capillary into the nephron, but they are absorbed back into the blood.

(ii) The **amount** of urea in the urine and blood is the same. However, it makes up a greater proportion of the urine (is more concentrated in urine), because smaller amounts of other substances are present, e.g. blood contains less protein and less glucose.

## Question 6
(a) Umbilical vein (because foetal blood picks up oxygen in the placenta and the umbilical vein carries oxygen back from the placenta).
(b) Waste products, e.g. carbon dioxide, urea.
(c) To make energy (by respiration)
(d) Folding increases the surface area, so transfer of materials is more efficient.

## Question 7
(a) (i)

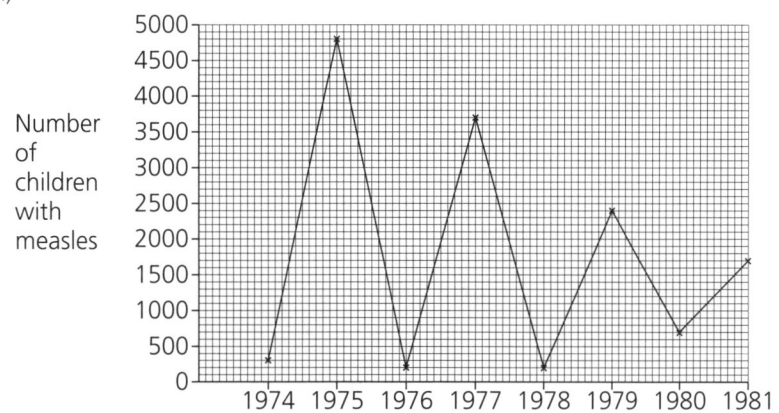

[1] for adding a scale to the vertical axis
   [2] for plotting points accurately
   [1] for joining the points with a line
 (ii) 1975
 (iii) A year with a high number of measles cases, e.g. 1975, 1977, 1979, is followed by a year with very few measles cases, e.g. 1976, 1978.
(b) (i) Acquired immunity.
 (ii) The child is vaccinated with **measles antigen**.
   White blood cells make **measles antibodies**.
   In the future, if the measles virus enters the child's body the **level of antibodies in the blood** will rise.
   This prevents the virus making the child ill – we say the child is **immune to this disease**.
 (iii) Breast milk contains antibodies made by the mother [1].
   They protect the baby by making it immune to the disease [1].

# 3 Green plants as organisms

## SOLUTION TO REVISION ACTIVITY

1 water + carbon dioxide $\xrightarrow{\text{light energy}}$ glucose + oxygen.

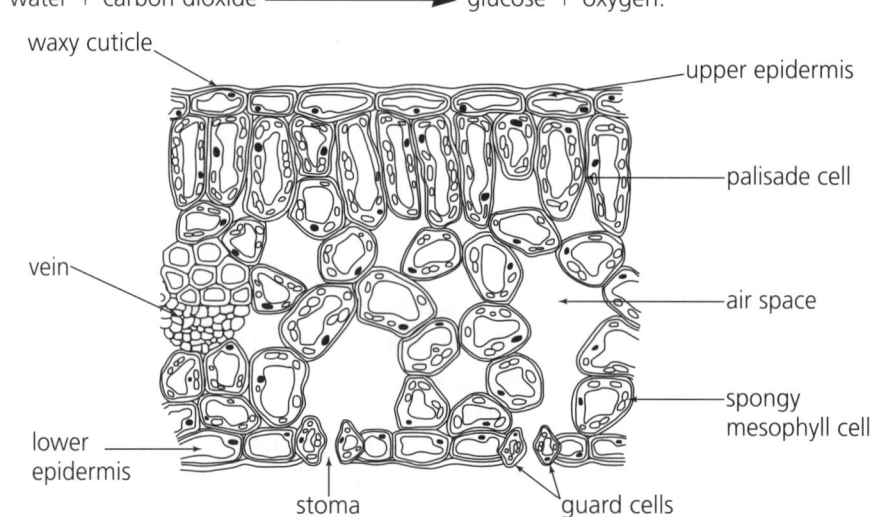

2 Diagram labelled: waxy cuticle, upper epidermis, palisade cell, vein, air space, spongy mesophyll cell, lower epidermis, stoma, guard cells.

3 Leaves are adapted for photosynthesis because they:
 (a) are thin and flat, so light reaches the photosynthesising cells
 (b) have chlorophyll to trap light
 (c) have stomata to allow gases to enter and leave
 (d) have veins to carry water and minerals to the leaf, and to carry sugar away
 (e) have veins help to support the leaf.

4 
| Part | Function |
| --- | --- |
| **palisade cells** | most photosynthesis occurs here |
| **xylem vessel** | carries water to the leaf |
| **upper epidermis** | makes the waxy cuticle to protect the leaf |
| **stoma** | pore to allow gases to enter and leave the leaf |
| **guard cells** | change shape to open and close the stomata |
| **phloem tube** | carries sugar away from the leaf |

5 Plants get the minerals they need from the **soil**. They are absorbed by **active** transport and **diffusion** in **root hair** cells which have a large **surface** area. They travel upwards through **xylem vessels** to all parts of the plant. Plants need a variety of

minerals, including **nitrate** to make protein and magnesium to make **chlorophyll**. If plants do not get the minerals they need, they will not grow properly and may look yellow. Farmers and gardeners can add extra minerals to the soil by digging in **fertilisers**.

6  (a) warm, light
   (b) Because in warm conditions water evaporates faster, and stomata are fully open in the light.
   (c) humidity and air movement (wind)
   (d) $\frac{7.2}{5}$ = 1.44 cm per minute
   (e) Lower, because transpiration stopped completely. Almost all stomata are found on the lower surface of the leaf, and when they were blocked with Vaseline transpiration stopped.

7  (a) auxins          (b) gibberellins        (c) ethene
   (d) cytokinins      (e) abscissic acid

## ANSWERS TO EXAMINATION QUESTIONS

### Question 1
(a) carbon dioxide + **water** ⟶ **glucose** + **oxygen**
(b) The area shown is 0.01 mm$^2$.
    It contains **11** stomata [1].
    An area 1 mm$^2$ is **100** times bigger than this, so it would contain 11 x 100 = **1100 stomata** [1].
(c) Each pore (stoma) is surrounded by two guard cells. The guard cells can change shape to open or close the stoma [1].
    If water is scarce, the guard cells close the stomata to reduce transpiration, i.e. slow down water loss [1].

### Question 2
(a) (i) It is used in photosynthesis [1] inside palisade cells [1] to make glucose and oxygen [1].
    (ii) Take a small plant, e.g. groundsel, and carefully wash soil off the roots [1]. Support the plant so that its roots are in a beaker of dye and leave it in a warm sunny place for 4–6 hours [1].
        Cut sections of the stem, and observe under a microscope – the dye in the water should be visible in the xylem vessels [1].
    (iii) Lignin
    (iv) When spongy mesophyll cells contain a lot of water, they are turgid [1]. (The vacuole is large and the cell membrane is pushed against the cell wall.) The cells press against each other, making the leaf firm but flexible [1].
    (v) There is a continuous column of water in the xylem vessels of a plant, running from roots to leaves [1]. When water vapour escapes through stomata, more water moves in through the root to replace it [1].
    This is called the transpiration stream [1].

(b)  **Examiner's note** Look at the number of marks available for this question, and try to make 5 separate points. Make sure you use the information you are given in the graph.

   (i) stomata are closed in the dark – from 9 p.m. (2100 hrs) to 3 a.m. (0300) hrs;
       stomata open slightly as it starts to get light;
       stomata begin to open fully at about 7 a.m. (0700 hrs);
       they are fully open by 10.30 a.m.;
       they close slightly from 10.30 a.m. to 6 p.m. (1800) hrs, perhaps due to short age of water.

(ii) When stomata are closed, less transpiration occurs [1] so the plant can conserve water and does not wilt [1]. Plants do this when water is scarce.

(iii) **Disadvantage**: gas exchange cannot occur, therefore photosynthesis may be reduced.
**Advantage**: less water is lost, so the plant will not wilt.

(iv) Each stoma is surrounded by two guard cells.
The walls of the guard cells are unevenly thickened with cellulose, so the cells curve when they become turgid.
If water moves into the guard cells by osmosis, the cells curve and the stoma is opened.
Water moves in due to increased amounts of sugar in the guard cells (made by photosynthesis during the day).
At night, guard cells cannot photosynthesise and sugar made during the day is used up (in respiration) so water moves out by osmosis.

**Question 3**

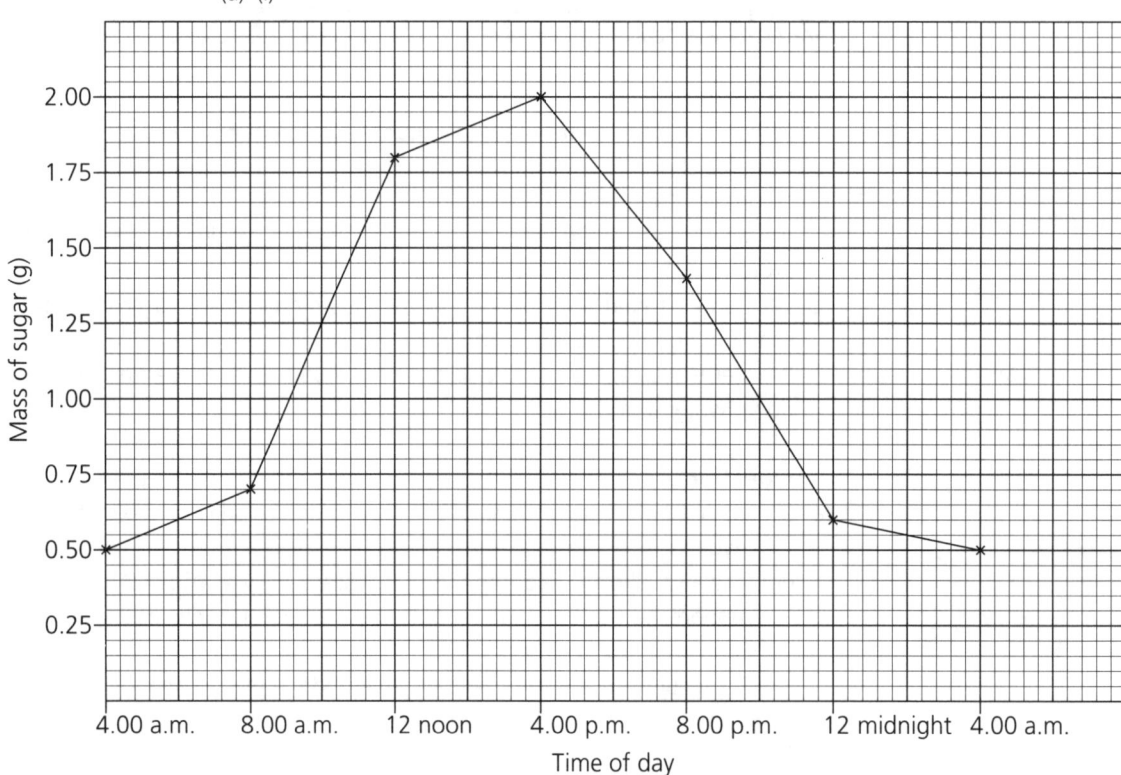

(a) (i)

[Graph: Mass of sugar (g) vs Time of day. Points plotted at 4.00 a.m. (0.50), 8.00 a.m. (0.70), 12 noon (1.80), 4.00 p.m. (2.00), 8.00 p.m. (1.40), 12 midnight (0.60), 4.00 a.m. (0.50).]

2 marks for adding suitable scales to the axes
1 mark for plotting points accurately
1 mark for joining points to make a line graph

(ii) Time = 4.00 p.m.
Explanation: Sugar has been made during the day by photosynthesis [1].
Excess sugar has accumulated in the leaf [1].

(iii) Sugar is being used by leaf cells [1] for respiration [1];
some sugar may be converted to starch for storage [1].

(b) (i)  1 low temperature         3 lack of carbon dioxide
         2 lack of light           4 lack of water

(ii) If another factor (apart from light) is in short supply, it acts as a limiting factor [1]. Lack of water or carbon dioxide or a cold temperature will slow down photosynthesis [1].

# 4 Variation, inheritance and evolution

## SOLUTION TO REVISION ACTIVITY

1 

| Named example | Scales? | Feathers? | Fur? | Fins? | Legs? | Lay eggs? | Breathe air? |
|---|---|---|---|---|---|---|---|
| Fish | ✓ | ✗ | ✗ | ✓ | ✗ | in water | ✗ |
| Amphibians | ✗ | ✗ | ✗ | ✗ | ✓ | in water | ✓ |
| Reptiles | ✓ | ✗ | ✗ | ✗ | some | on land | ✓ |
| Birds | ✗ | ✓ | ✗ | ✗ | ✓ | on land | ✓ |
| Mammals | ✗ | ✗ | ✓ | ✗ | some | no | ✓ |

2 (a) spider      (b) fern      (c) insect
  (d) sea mammal, e.g. whale, dolphin, porpoise, seal, etc.
  (e) mollusc, e.g. snail

3 Scutigerella

4 (a) Contains half the number of chromosomes in a body cell.
  (b) When two haploid gametes fuse, the zygote is diploid, i.e. it contains the correct number of chromosomes.
  (c) Meiosis
  (d)

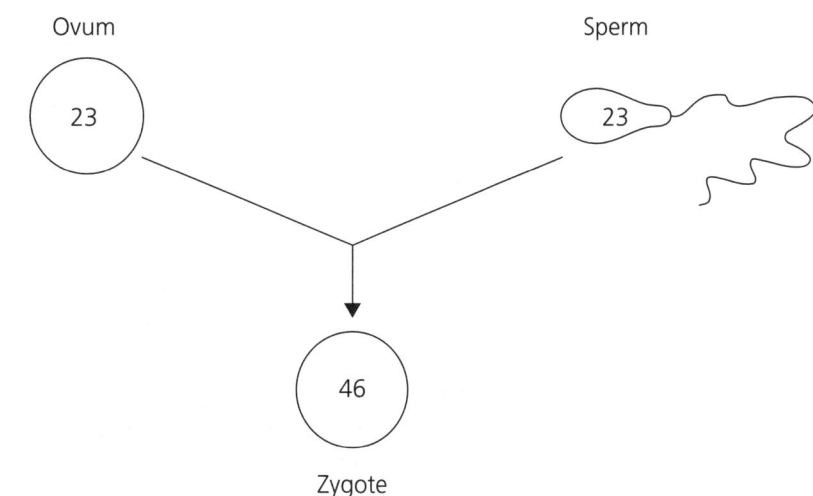

Ovum (23)      Sperm (23)

→ Zygote (46)

5 (a) **chromosome**: Long piece of DNA containing thousands of genes.
    **gene**: Part of a chromosome. A short piece of DNA carrying information to make one protein.
  (b) **genotype**: The genes an individual has.
    **phenotype**: The appearance/characteristics of an individual.
  (c) **homozygous**: An individual who has two identical alleles, e.g. BB or bb.
    **heterozygous**: An individual who has two different alleles, e.g. Bb.

6 Parents: tall plant (Tt)      dwarf plant (tt)

Gametes: T, t      t, t

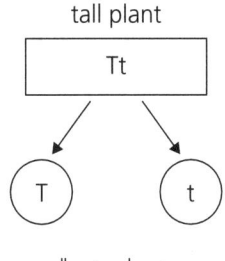

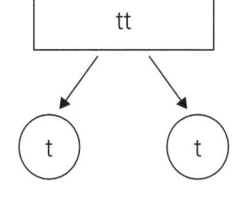

F1:

|   | t  | t  |
|---|----|----|
| T | Tt | Tt |
| t | tt | tt |

Tt = tall plant
Tt = tall plant
tt = dwarf plant
tt = dwarf plant

**Phenotypes**: Half will be tall, half will be dwarf
**Ratio**: 1:1

**7** The probability of a boy being colourblind is 0.5 (50%).
The probability of a girl being colourblind is nil.

Parents        $X^R X^r$        $X^R Y$

Gametes        $(X^R)\ (X^r)$        $(X^R)\ (Y)$

|          | $(X^R)$   | $(Y)$   |
|----------|-----------|---------|
| $(X^R)$  | $X^R X^R$ | $X^R Y$ |
| $(X^r)$  | $X^R X^r$ | $X^r Y$ |

$X^R X^R$ = normal girl
$X^R X^r$ = normal girl (carrier)
$X^R Y$ = normal boy
$X^r Y$ = colourblind boy

**8**

A = adenine
G = guanine
T = thymine
C = cytosine

DNA is a **double helix** because it is formed of **two** strands of nucleotides, twisted into a **spiral** shape.

**9** In any species, there is **variation** between individuals, i.e. they are not all identical. This is partly due to the **genes** they inherit from their parents and to mutation. Mutation is a mistake in copying **DNA** when the cell divides, and the chance of this happening is increased by **mutagens**, e.g. radiation or **chemicals**. When resources are scarce, individuals have to **compete** to survive. Some individuals are better suited to their environment so they will survive, but others will **die**. The survivors will **breed** and will have offspring like themselves. Gradually, changes will build up and we say that **evolution** has occurred. One example of natural selection involves peppered moths which rest on lichen-covered tree trunks. In rural areas, the trunks are **pale** coloured, so the moths are well camouflaged. In industrial areas, **gases** have killed the lichens and the trunks are darkened by soot. Here pale moths are not well camouflaged, so they are eaten by **birds**. Mutant **dark** moths are much more likely to survive.

## ANSWERS TO EXAMINATION QUESTIONS

### Question 1
(a) 2 kingdoms (Fungi and Plants)
(b) D = Liverwort
Sequence: 1, 4, 5

### Question 2
(a) **Growth, Movement, Respiration, Excretion**
(b) (i) Both lay eggs in water;
Both are cold-blooded (ectothermic);
Both have external fertilisation.
(ii) Scaly skin helps them to avoid water loss;
Lungs allow them to breathe air;

# answers and grading

Internal fertilisation allows sperm to swim to egg (through fluid in the female reproductive system);
They lay small numbers of eggs in a nest, or bury them in sand/vegetation to keep them at the right temperature.
(iii) Fish – Gills, swim bladder
Birds – Feathers, wings

## Question 3

(a) (i) 3 pupils out of 12, i.e. $\frac{1}{4}$ are left handed
4 pupils out of 12, i.e. $\frac{1}{3}$, are over 160 cm tall.
(ii) Ability to roll the tongue, and right/left handed are examples of discontinuous variation.
(iii) In continuous variation, there is a **range** of values between the greatest and the least [1]. Height and shoe size are examples of this [1].
(iv) Most pupils will have grown taller and will have bigger feet.

(b) (i) A mutation is a mistake made when DNA is copying itself (replicating) [1]. This can happen during cell division [1]. It leads to faulty genes [1].
(ii) A sperm cell with a mutation will have changed one or more genes [1]. These genes are passed on to his children, so they will have inherited different genes to normal, i.e. this increases variation [1].

## Question 4

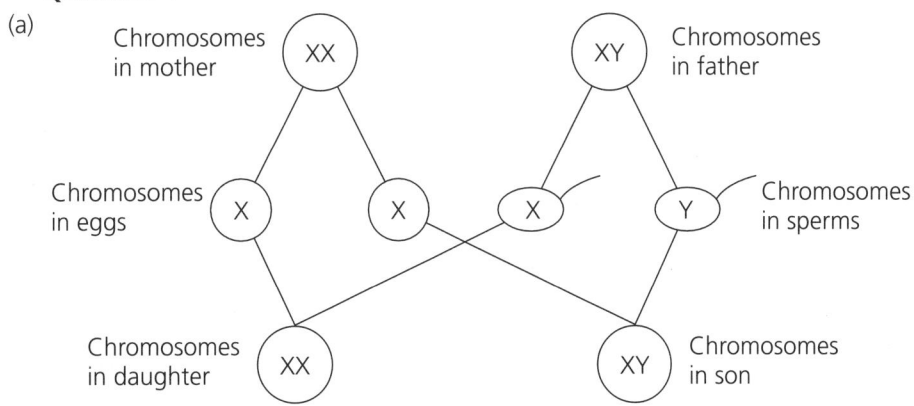

(a)

Chromosomes in mother: XX
Chromosomes in father: XY
Chromosomes in eggs: X, X
Chromosomes in sperms: X, Y
Chromosomes in daughter: XX
Chromosomes in son: XY

(b) 1  Chance of G developing disease = 50%
2  Chance of H developing disease = 0%

**Explanation**
- Huntington's chorea is an autosomal dominant disease:
  i.e. **HH** = affected          **H** = allele for Huntington's chorea
  **Hh** = affected          **h** = allele for normal
  **hh** = not affected
- Sufferers will probably have shown symptoms by the age of 40, so we can tell who is affected in generations 1 and 2.
- A is not a sufferer, so is **hh**.
- B is a sufferer, so could be **HH** or **Hh**. Some of B's children are not affected, e.g. E, so B **must** be **Hh**.
- C is not affected (**hh**), D must be **Hh** (because he has inherited **h** from his mother and **H** from his father).

| Parents | C | D | Their child (G) has an equal |
|---|---|---|---|
|  | hh | Hh | chance of being affected (**Hh**) |
| Gametes | (h) (h) | (H) (h) | or unaffected(**hh**). |

|  | (H) | (h) |
|---|---|---|
| (h) | Hh | hh |
| (h) | Hh | hh |

– E and F are both unaffected (hh). All of their children will be unaffected.

Parents         E               F
                    hh             hh
Gametes   (h) (h)    (h) (h)

|     | (h) | (h) |
|-----|-----|-----|
| (h) | hh  | hh  |
| (h) | hh  | hh  |

## Question 5

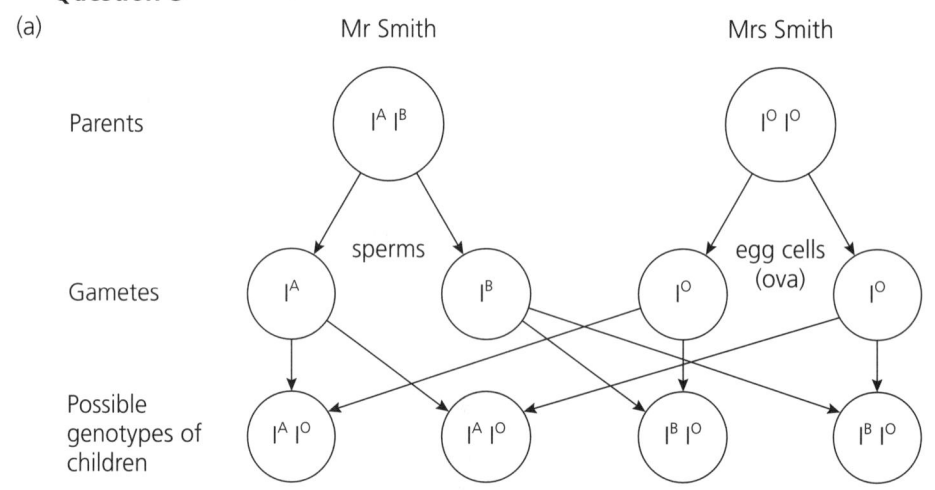

(a)

Mr Smith $I^A I^B$      Mrs Smith $I^O I^O$

Gametes (sperms): $I^A$, $I^B$    Gametes (egg cells/ova): $I^O$, $I^O$

Possible genotypes of children: $I^A I^O$, $I^A I^O$, $I^B I^O$, $I^B I^O$

(b) incomplete dominance, or co-dominance

(c) (i) 0.5 (50%)                  (ii) 0.25 (25%)

(d) Mrs Smith, because she is blood group O and this does not cause the production of antigen on red blood cells.

## Question 6

(a) 

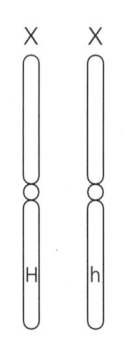

Two X chromosomes, one labelled H and one labelled h.

1 mark for drawing two X chromosomes
1 mark for labelling the alleles H and h (so she is a carrier)

(b) (i) Mr Smith = $X^h Y$     Mrs Smith = $X^H X^h$

**Explanation**
– John is affected ($X^h Y$); he must have inherited $X^h$ from his mother, and Y from his father.
– Julie is affected ($X^h X^h$); she must have inherited $X^h$ from her mother and $X^h$ from her father, **therefore**, Mr Smith is $X^h Y$.
– Jason is unaffected ($X^H Y$); he must have inherited $X^H$ from his mother and Y from his father, **therefore**, Mrs Smith is $X^H X^h$ (a carrier).

(ii) Probability = 0
**Explanation**: An affected female is $X^h X^h$.
Ann is a carrier ($X^H X^h$) but Peter is unaffected ($X^H Y$) so he cannot pass on $X^h$ to a daughter.

(c) **Examiner's note** You are not expected to be familiar with this information but you should be able to use the facts you are given to answer the question.

1 Thrombokinase could be faulty.
2 Prothrombin could be faulty.

3 Fibrinogen could be faulty.
4 Heparin could be faulty.

***Examiner's note*** **NOT** faulty calcium ions (they are not made by genes); nor faulty thrombin or fibrin (these are made **during** the clotting process, they are not present initially).

## Question 7

(a) X = Thymine   Look at the shape at the end of the symbols;
Y = Cytosine   X matches Adenine, Y matches Guanine.

(b) Process = replication [1]
There are five marks available for describing replication.
You could include any of these points:
- DNA starts to unwind;
- because hydrogen bonds between bases break;
- new bases (or nucleotides) line up against unpaired bases;
- Adenine bonds to Thymine;
- Cytosine bonds to Guanine;
- the new bases are joined by an enzyme (DNA polymerase);
- to form two identical molecules of DNA;
- each molecule of DNA is made up of one original strand and one newly formed strand.

(c) The bases are read in groups of three (triplet or codon) [1].
Each triplet codes for one amino acid [1].
So the correct amino acids are put together in the correct order [1].

## Question 8

(a) (i) Humans select organisms (plants or animals) with useful characteristics [1].
They breed these organisms together [1].
They choose offspring who have the desired characteristics and breed these together [1].
They continue to repeat these steps until they have obtained offspring with the mixture of characteristics they require.
(ii) disease resistance/high yield/high nutritional value/height

(b) (i) Hh        (ii) All of them
(iii) $\frac{3}{4}$ would be tall and $\frac{1}{4}$ would be short [1].
Parents are both heterozygous (Hh) [1].
Offspring will be HH, Hh, Hh, hh [1].
**or** draw a genetic cross including a Punnett square to answer this question.
(iv) The F1 hybrid has known parents, so it is likely to have good features, e.g. tall, disease-resistant. The parents of freely pollinated plants are unknown, so their characteristics are unknown.
(v) The white plant is a mutant [1].
The gene for chlorophyll is faulty [1] because a mistake was made when the DNA for this gene was being copied [1].
(vi) It will not be able to photosynthesise properly due to lack of chlorophyll [1].
It will not grow well (because less sugar is available for respiration); it will probably die [1].

(c) (i) A useful gene from another organism (the donor) [1], is transferred into an organism (the recipient) [1], so the recipient has new characteristics [1].
(ii) They can use nitrogen gas to make proteins [1], so fertilisers do not have to be used [1]. This saves money [1].
(iii) Genetically engineered plants can escape into the environment [1], where they compete with natural plants [1] and disrupt food webs [1].
They should be isolated from natural plants [1].

### Question 9

A useful gene is identified      D

The gene is cut out of the donor DNA      F

The gene is inserted into a vector organism      E

The vector transfers the useful gene to the cell of a crop plant      B

The crop plant cell is cloned to produce many transgenic plants      C

The new transgenic crop plants undergo trials to find out if the useful gene has the desired effect.      A

# 5 Living organisms in their environment

## SOLUTION TO REVISION ACTIVITY

1. (a) Dry, exposed, hot during the day, cold at night.
   (b) Spines – less likely to be eaten by herbivores.
   Fleshy stem – stores water, can photosynthesise.
   Deep root – to absorb any available water.
2. (a) Fox.
   (b) There were too few rabbits to eat, i.e. food was scarce, so some foxes died.
   (c) The number of foxes was high, so a lot of rabbits were being eaten.
   (d) Foxes would decrease, because their food source would decrease.
3. (a) lack of food, lack of space
   (b) dotted line on graph
   (c) disease, poor weather conditions, pollution
4. (a) sulphur dioxide     (e) oil pollution
   (b) carbon monoxide     (f) carbon dioxide
   (c) CFCs     (g) accumulation of pesticides
   (d) fertiliser run-off     (h) dumping of untreated sewage.
5. (a) woodland or grassland
   (b) (i) oak tree, grass     (ii) caterpillar, rabbit, grasshopper
   (iii) owl, fox, weasel, badger     (iv) tick, flea
   (v) caterpillar, rabbit, grasshopper     (vi) shrew, fox, weasel, badger
   (c) the Sun.
6. (a) Pyramid B     (b) fleas / owl / shrews / caterpillars / oak tree

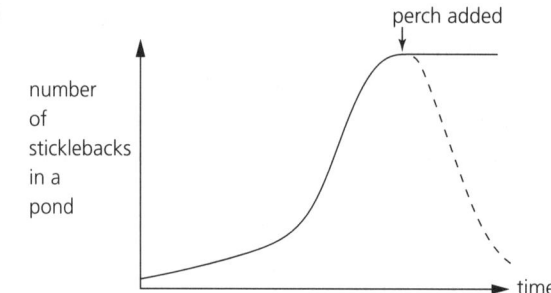

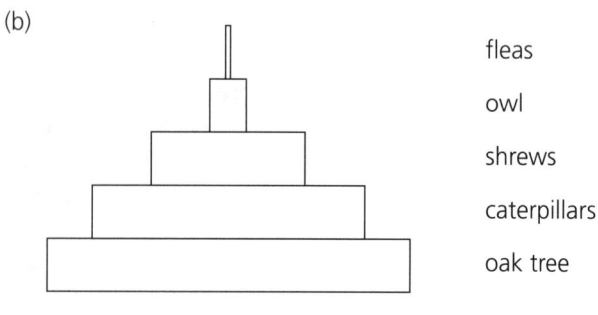

# answers and grading

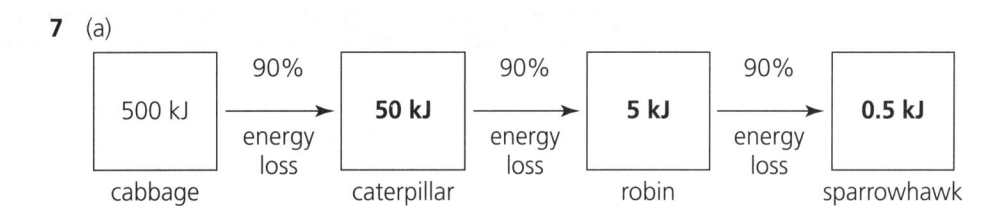

7 (a)

```
┌─────────┐  90%    ┌─────────┐  90%    ┌─────────┐  90%    ┌─────────┐
│  500 kJ │ ──────► │  50 kJ  │ ──────► │  5 kJ   │ ──────► │ 0.5 kJ  │
└─────────┘ energy  └─────────┘ energy  └─────────┘ energy  └─────────┘
  cabbage    loss    caterpillar loss      robin    loss    sparrowhawk
```

(b) Each organism uses about 10% of its energy intake to make structures inside the body, e.g. protein, fat, and this can be passed on. It uses about 90% of its energy intake in movement, keeping warm and vital processes – this energy cannot be passed on to other organisms.

(c) Each trophic level has less biomass than the level before, so a pyramid of biomass is triangular, with a broad base.

8

|   | light | wet | air available | temperature | decay fast/slow /not at all | reason |
|---|---|---|---|---|---|---|
| 1 | yes | yes | no  | 25°C | not at all | air is needed |
| 2 | yes | no  | yes | 25°C | not at all | water is needed |
| 3 | no  | yes | yes | 25°C | fast       | temperature is warm, light is not necessary |
| 4 | yes | yes | yes | 10°C | slowly     | temperature is colder (microbes work slowly) |
| 5 | yes | yes | yes | 2°C  | not at all | temperature is too cold |
| 6 | no  | no  | yes | 37°C | not at all | water is needed |
| 7 | yes | yes | no  | 37°C | not at all | air is needed |
| 8 | no  | no  | no  | 37°C | not at all | water and air needed |

9 A = **combustion**  B = **respiration**  C = **photosynthesis**  D = **decay**  E = **feeding**

10 Although the air is made up of 79% **nitrogen** gas, most organisms cannot use it. **Nitrogen fixing** bacteria live in root **nodules** of some plants, e.g. peas and **beans/clover**, or they live free in the soil, and they can change **nitrogen** into nitrates. Nitrates are absorbed by plant roots and used inside plants to make **proteins**. When plants are eaten by **animals/herbivores**, proteins containing nitrogen are transferred. Dead animals and plants and their waste products, e.g. urine, faeces, are broken down by **decomposers** to form ammonium compounds. **Nitrifying** bacteria change ammonium compounds into nitrates which plants can use. Farmers can add extra nitrate to the soil by digging **fertilisers** into it.

11 (a) **Increased temperature** because photosynthesis is enzyme dependent, and occurs faster at warmer temperatures.

(b) **Increased light** because light provides the energy for the photosynthesis reaction to occur.

(c) **Plenty of water** because water is needed as a reactant in photosynthesis and plants wilt and close their stomata if they are short of water.

(d) **Increased carbon dioxide** because it is a reactant in photosynthesis (carbon dioxide is fixed to make carbohydrate.)

(e) **Add minerals** (fertiliser) because plants need minerals to make proteins, chlorophyll, DNA and other important compounds.

(f) **Exclude pests** (using pesticides or biological control) because pests will decrease crop yield by causing disease or by taking nutrients the plant would use for growth.

Farmers keep bees in greenhouses to pollinate the plants and increase crop yield (of fruits).

# ANSWERS TO EXAMINATION QUESTIONS

### Question 1
(a) (i) To attract the slugs/to act as a bait.
 (ii) So the slugs could not climb out once they had got into the jars.
 (iii) To keep rain out (so the slugs would not drown).
  To stop predators, e.g. birds, from seeing the slugs and killing them in the trap.
(b) Average number of slugs per trap in the vegetable garden
$$= 0 + 10 + 14 + 5 + 26 = \frac{55}{5} = \mathbf{11}$$
(c) (i) There are more plants in the vegetable garden (28 compared with 11 in the flower beds).
  Slugs may prefer the leaves of vegetable plants.
  Slugs can hide between the vegetable plants; in the flower garden there are large areas of lawn where they cannot hide, so they are more likely to be eaten by predators.
 (ii) Give a large number of slugs a choice of which type of leaves to eat by putting out two dishes; one with vegetable leaves and one with flower leaves.
(d) It gives you more accurate results [1] because different traps have different numbers of slugs, even in the same part of the garden [1].
 It could be due to chance, or due to other factors, e.g. sunniness, dampness, etc.[1]
(e) Spread out the traps in the flower garden more evenly.
 Place the traps more randomly in both parts of the garden.
 Put the traps out again to repeat the experiment and collect more results.

### Question 2
(a) Two marks for plotting points accurately
 One mark for joining the points to make a line graph

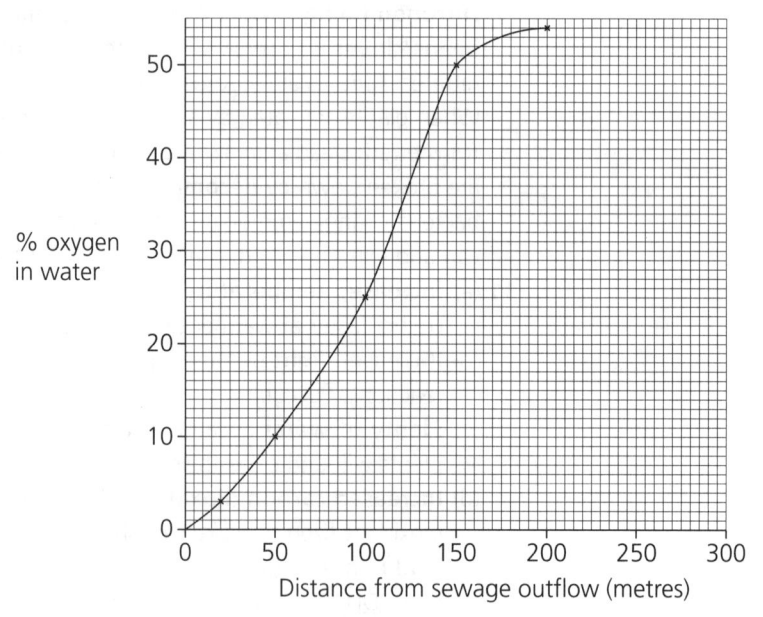

[Graph: % oxygen in water vs Distance from sewage outflow (metres), showing a sigmoid curve rising from 0 near the outflow to above 50% at 300 m]

(b) Oxygen concentration rises as the water flows away from the outflow.
(c) Calculate this figure by reading it from the graph = 37%.
(d) Fish (they are only found when there is more than 50% dissolved oxygen).
(e) (i) Bacteria or fungi.
 (ii) Decomposition–they use up oxygen when they break down sewage.
 (iii) 0–20 m, i.e. closest to the outflow.
(f) Air passes from the atmosphere through the breathing tube/tail into its body.
 It breathes air, it does not get oxygen from the water.
(g) (i) How energy passes along the food chain/how food passes from one organism to another as they are eaten.

(ii) Microscopic algae.
(iii) They would increase (because the insects would eat more water fleas, so less algae would be eaten by water fleas).

## Question 3

(a) 1  Pesticides can be passed along food chains and can harm other organisms, e.g. top carnivores; this does not happen with biological control.
2  Pesticides can be washed off crops and into rivers where they pollute water and harm aquatic animals; this does not happen with biological control.
3  Pesticide residues may remain on crops eaten by humans – biological control organisms do not affect humans.
4  Biological control methods are specific (they kill only the pest); pesticides may kill many useful organisms as well as the pest.
5  Biological control is cheaper than using pesticides; the control organism will breed naturally, but pesticides need to be continually reapplied.

(b) (i) Sulphur dioxide
(ii) Amount of sulphur dioxide on outskirts = 200 micrograms/m$^3$
Amount of sulphur dioxide in city centre = 65 micrograms/m$^3$
difference = 200 − 65
   = 135 micrograms/m$^3$ of air.
(iii) 3 km from city centre.
(iv) The lime neutralises the acid in acid rain [1], so more lichens can grow on walls than on trees or in grassland [1].

## Question 4

(a) There are lots of possible answers to this. Remember, a food chain must always start with a producer (plant).
e.g.  leaf litter ⟶ earthworms ⟶ beetles ⟶ shrews
      oak trees ⟶ other leaf eaters ⟶ beetles ⟶ shrews
      oak trees ⟶ moths ⟶ beetles ⟶ shrews
      trees/bushes ⟶ moths ⟶ beetles ⟶ shrews

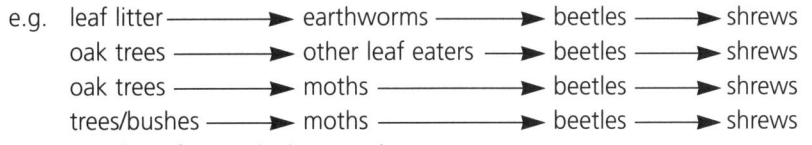

(b) If the number of weasels decreased:
Fewer small birds would be eaten; so numbers of small birds would increase.
Number of moths would decrease, because more would be eaten by small birds.

(c) (i) Voles/small birds/beetles (this is the third trophic level of the web).
(ii) Level Y is the producers.
In a wood, many of the plants are very large (trees), so in 0.1 hectare, you would expect a small **number** of plants.
BUT each tree is a large organism containing a lot of organic matter, so it has a high biomass.
A pyramid of biomass has a wide base because it takes account of the **size** of organisms, not just the number.

(d) (i) Decomposers living in the soil (bacteria and fungi) broke down the leaf litter by feeding on it.
(ii) Decomposition was fastest in March because the temperature was increasing. Decomposers work faster when it is warm.
(iii) **There are six marks available for this answer, and you need to be clear about the steps of the nitrogen cycle before you begin.**
Protein in leaf litter is broken down by decomposers;
Ammonia is produced;
Ammonia is broken down by nitrifying bacteria;
Nitrate is produced;
Plant roots absorb nitrate;
It travels through xylem vessels in plants to the leaf;
Nitrate is used to make proteins.

You could also obtain marks by giving named examples of the bacteria involved.

## Question 5

This question **looks** very difficult, so you need to approach it one part at a time.
Check answers to the calculations carefully to avoid making silly mistakes.

(a) (i) Photosynthesis

(ii) Total energy reaching pond = 6 400 000 kJ
Energy fixed = 32 000 kJ

% energy fixed = $\frac{32\,000}{6\,400\,000} \times 100$ = **0.5%**

(iii) It could:
be reflected off the pond surface;
fall on a part of the pond where there are no plants;
be the wrong wavelength to be absorbed by plants.

No marks available for:
Heat up the water – because the question refers to *light* energy.
Used in plant respiration – because that information is already on the flow chart at the next level.

(b) 32 000 kJ is fixed by pond plants.
Of this; 6400 kJ is used for respiration,
20 480 kJ is consumed by herbivores.
So amount of energy not consumed
= 32 000 − 20 480 + 6400
= 32 000 − 26 880
= **5120 kJ**

(c) Herbivores release much more energy by respiration (about twice as much) because they use energy moving around.

(d) Faeces are broken down (eaten) by other organisms, e.g. bacteria/fungi; the energy passes to these organisms (called decomposers).

(e) The only way that energy can pass along a food chain is by organisms being eaten (or decomposed).
The two possibilities are:
1 Aquatic **plants** are eaten by land animals, so energy passes into the land-based food chain.
2 Aquatic **animals** are eaten by land animals, e.g. birds catching fish, humans catching fish.

## Question 6

(a) **Glucose/sugar/carbohydrate** + oxygen → carbon dioxide + **water** + **energy**

(b) (i) Mass of carbon removed from the atmosphere each year includes:
Amount removed by photosynthesis = 100 billion tonnes
Amount removed by biological and chemical absorption
= 104 billion tonnes.
Total = **204 billion tonnes**

(ii) Percentage removed by photosynthesis = $\frac{100}{204} \times 100$ = **49.02%**

(c) Warm water contains less dissolved oxygen, so some organisms will die, e.g. fish.
All animals living in rivers are cold blooded, so their body temperature will rise if warm water is added.
When their body temperature rises, they need more oxygen to stay alive (because metabolic rate rises). If there is not enough oxygen available, they will die.
Warm water will make many organisms more active, and they may grow faster.

(d) (i) 1 Increased use of motor vehicles, e.g. for leisure, commuting, transport of goods.
2 Increased use in power stations, to make electricity to power domestic appliances and for industry.
3 Increased use by industry as manufacturing processes become more complex.

(ii) 1 Higher levels of carbon dioxide: linked to the greenhouse effect and global warming.
2 Higher levels of sulphur dioxide: linked to acid rain.
3 Higher levels of carbon monoxide/nitrogen oxides/soot.
4 Environmental damage from mining/drilling/oil spills, etc.

(iii) Trees use carbon dioxide when they photosynthesise.
Cutting down/burning trees kills trees and reduces photosynthesis, so less carbon dioxide is removed from the air, and levels rise.
When trees are burned, carbon dioxide is released as a waste product of combustion.

(e) 1 Increased dumping of rubbish in landfill sites. It releases methane when it decomposes.
2 Increased breakdown of sewage by bacteria (in sewage treatment plants). It releases methane when it decomposes.

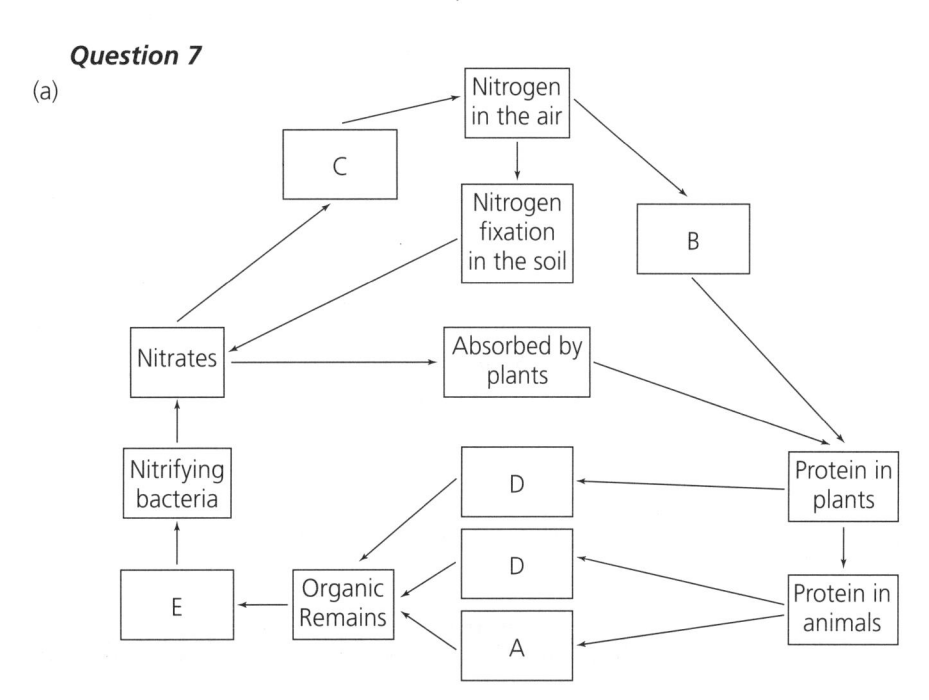

## Question 7

(a) [Nitrogen cycle diagram with boxes labelled: Nitrogen in the air, C, Nitrogen fixation in the soil, B, Nitrates, Absorbed by plants, Nitrifying bacteria, D, Protein in plants, E, Organic Remains, D, A, Protein in animals]

(b) It would not be able to make proteins, so it would not grow properly, and may die.

(c) (i) Because the Earth contains a limited amount of nitrogen, so it must be re-used.
All living things need nitrogen to make proteins.

(ii) 1 respiration   2 decomposition   3 combustion

## Question 8

(a) Chemical = fertiliser
**Explanation**: If there are no pests, there is no need for insecticide, herbicide or fungicide. Fertiliser adds minerals to the soil, so plants grow better and crop yield will be higher.

(b) 1 Remove couch grass (a weed)    3 Use a fungicide chemical
2 Plough stubble into the soil    4 Crop rotation

(c) (i) The couch grass uses minerals and water from the soil, so the crop plant does not grow as well.
The couch grass may shade the crop plant, so it has less light for photosynthesis and does not grow properly.

(ii) Herbicide

(d) (i) The plant turns yellow because it contains less chlorophyll.
This leads to reduced photosynthesis (chlorophyll traps light), so the plant makes less sugar.
It has less energy available for growth.

(ii) It is carried by a vector, e.g. beet aphid.

(iii) Use an insecticide to kill aphids. They will no longer carry viruses to the crop.
(e) Residues of chemicals remaining in food crops and being passed on to humans.
Residues of chemicals being washed into rivers and harming the environment.
Safety of agricultural workers who are exposed to high levels of chemicals.

### Question 9

There are two marks available for each part of this question. You must show you understand the significance of the part labelled, and how it will improve yield.

A  Insulated room maintains a high temperature.
Prawns are cold blooded (ectothermic) so their body temperature is the same as their environmental temperature.
They will grow faster when it is warm (they have a higher metabolic rate).

B  Filter cleans the water so it can be recycled.
Micro-organisms remove organic matter, e.g. faeces, uneaten food particles, so the tank does not become polluted.
The micro-organisms are decomposers.

C  Food is added to the tank for prawns.
This is high in protein and energy to increase growth rate.
Amount of food is carefully calculated to maximise growth rate and minimise waste.

D  Aeration unit bubbles air through the tank.
Prawns need oxygen for respiration (to make energy for growth).
This allows large numbers of prawns to be kept in a small space without running out of oxygen.

# 6 Extension topics

## SOLUTION TO REVISION ACTIVITY

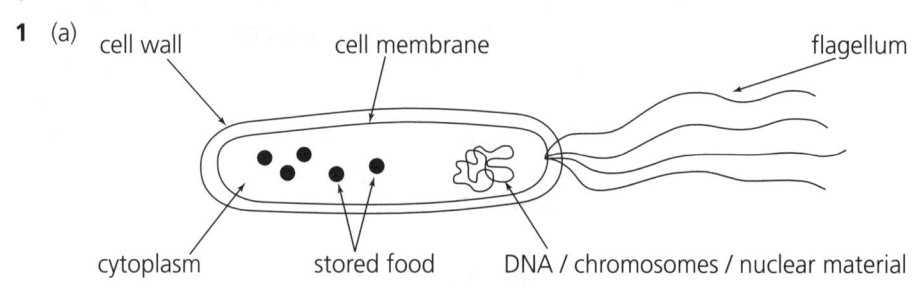

1 (a) Labelled diagram of a bacterium: cell wall, cell membrane, flagellum, cytoplasm, stored food, DNA / chromosomes / nuclear material

(b) (i) the bacterium has a cell wall, the virus does not
(ii) the bacterium has a cell membrane, the virus does not
(iii) the bacterium has cytoplasm, the virus does not
(iv) the bacterium is much bigger than the virus
(v) the bacterium carries out the 7 basic life processes, the virus does not

(c) virus, bacterium, yeast, mould

2 (a) (i) Cooling jacket – water circulates through this to reduce the temperature (microbes make heat when they respire).
(ii) Stirrer – stops microbes, food particles, etc. sinking to the bottom of the fermenter.
(iii) Air line – most microbes need oxygen for respiration.

(b) Optimum temperature = 25–40°C.
Metabolism in microbes is enzyme dependent; enzymes work faster in this range, so yield will be higher.

# answers and grading

3  (a) bacteria:  vinegar, binary fission
   (b) yeast:     budding, brewing
   (c) viruses:   capsid, replication
   (d) moulds:    hyphae, mycoprotein

4  (a) Cold temperatures stop bacteria reproducing rapidly.
   (b) If the middle of food, e.g. chicken, is frozen, it may not be heated enough during cooking to kill bacteria, so live bacteria may be eaten.
   (c) If raw meat is stored at the top of the fridge, meat juices may drip on to other foods and contaminate them with bacteria.
   (d) Bread is eaten uncooked. If it is cut with a knife/board which has been used for raw meat and not cleaned properly, food poisoning could occur.
   (e) Bacteria can multiply very fast in dishcloths (they are warm and damp and contain food waste). They should be boiled to kill bacteria, or replaced.

5  (a) It uses a raw material (plant waste) which would otherwise be thrown away.
   (b) It is relatively cheap to produce.
   (c) It conserves petrol resources, and reduces environmental damage from oil drilling/refining.
   (d) It is a 'clean fuel', i.e. does not contain impurities which increase air pollution.

6  (a) **A D E C B**
   (b) An enzyme called rennin is needed to make cheese. This is obtained from calves' stomachs and it solidifies milk proteins so they can be separated from the milk. Bacteria are given the gene to make rennin.
   Rennin from bacteria is used in the manufacture of cheese.
   Vegetarians can eat it because it is not harmful to animals.

7  (a) Diagram labels: A, biceps muscle, shoulder blade, humerus, triceps muscle, B, radius, ulna
   (b) If tendons stretched, they would get longer when muscles contract and bones would not move, so tendons must be inelastic.
   (c) A = ball and socket joint
   B = hinge joint

8  (a) A tropism = a growth movement in plants in response to a stimulus.
   (b) Geotropic = response to gravity. Negatively geotropic means that shoots grow away from gravity, i.e. they grow upwards.
   (c) Correct answer = **5**
   Reason:
   Shoot A is intact and will respond properly, i.e. bend towards the light, because auxin is produced at the tip.
   Shoot B has the tip covered, so it cannot detect the light and does not produce auxin, so it does not bend.
   Shoot C has the tip removed, so it cannot detect the light and does not produce auxin, so it does not bend.
   Auxin causes bending by making some cells grow faster (elongate more) than others.

## ANSWERS TO EXAMINATION QUESTIONS

### Question 1
(a) A = virus    B = bacterium    C = yeast
(b) Viruses are smaller than bacteria
(c) Yeast is a fungus
(d) A virus can be grown in a laboratory in hens' eggs.

## Question 2

(a) It would be best to stop after 120 hours because the concentration of antibiotic does not change after that time, i.e. that is the maximum level.

(b) Add more food to the fermenter.
Add more fungus to the fermenter.

(c) (i) Bacteria      (ii) By coughing/sneezing

(d) Antibiotics are used more often now than in 1950, so bacteria have become used to them. Some bacteria are resistant, or are only killed by larger doses.

(e) If bacteria become resistant, the drugs we have now will not work. Scientists will have to develop new drugs to kill bacteria.

(f) 1  Better hygiene from infected people, e.g. do not cough or sneeze over other people, always cover your face/use a handkerchief.
   2  Vaccinate people against streptococcal infections.

## Question 3

(a) (i) Bacteria (lactic acid bacteria)
   (ii) Bacteria change lactose (sugar) into lactic acid
   (iii) Proteins are denatured and become insoluble, so the milk separates into lumpy curds and liquid whey.

(b) (i) **There are five marks available for this section, so you must summarise the key points of genetic engineering in an organised way**.
   The gene for rennin is identified and removed from calf cells.
   It is cut out of the calf DNA using an enzyme (restriction enzyme).
   It is joined on to a plasmid (small circular piece of DNA).
   The plasmid acts as a vector to get the calf gene into the bacterium.
   The bacterium absorbs the plasmid and copies are made.
   The bacterium has the gene for rennin and can make this enzyme.
   The bacterium can be transferred to a fermenter where it will produce lots of offspring (by asexual reproduction, so they are all identical): this is cloning.
   (ii) They are worried that it is not safe or pure, because it has been made by bacteria.
   They are worried that it is not natural, because humans have interfered with bacterial genes.
   They are worried that mutations may occur, making the bacteria dangerous.
   (iii) Large amounts of rennin can be produced very cheaply.
   Calves do not have to be killed to obtain rennin.
   Vegetarians can eat the cheese, since it has not involved harm to animals.

(c) (i) Bacteria (acetic acid bacteria)
   (ii) Nutrients, e.g. air, wine, are continuously added to the fermenter.
   Product, i.e. vinegar, is continuously removed from fermenter.
   The fermenter runs for a long period of time without being stopped.
   (iii) The bacteria need oxygen for respiration (they are aerobic).
   The shavings fit into the fermenter so there are air pockets between them.
   Air bubbles up from the base of the fermenter through the air pockets, so bacteria come into contact with the air.
   Without the shavings, all the bacteria would form a layer at the base of the fermenter and it would be hard for air to penetrate.
   (iv) Oxidation (ethanol + oxygen → ethanoic acid + water)
   ethanoic acid = vinegar.
   (v) This process is controlled by enzymes [1].
   It will be faster at warm temperatures [1], but bacteria will be killed if they get too hot [1].

## Question 4

(a) (i) scurvy      (ii) common cold      (iii) athlete's foot

(b) 1  Antiseptics kill bacteria outside the body, e.g. kitchen surfaces, drains, etc.; antibiotics kill bacteria inside the body.

2 Antiseptics are strong chemicals made industrially; antibiotics are natural products made by fungi.

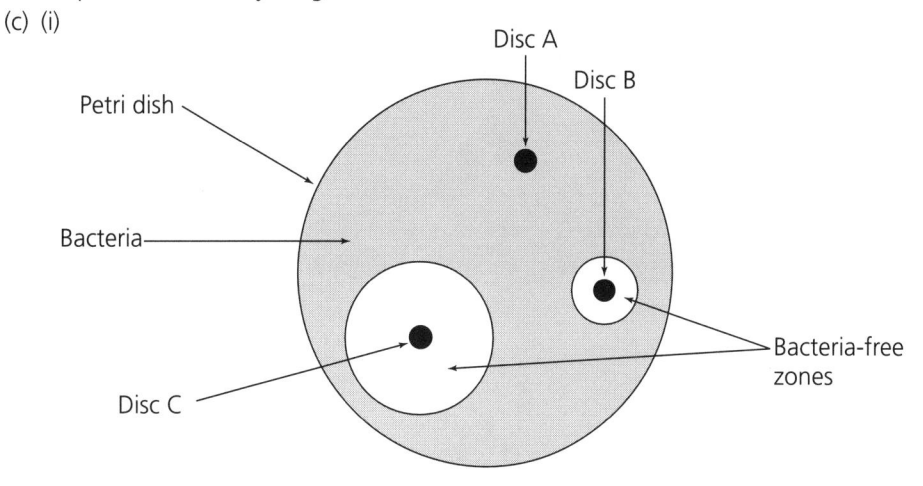

(c) (i)

*[Diagram of Petri dish showing Disc A at top with small bacteria-free zone, Disc B to the right with small bacteria-free zone, and Disc C at bottom with large bacteria-free zone, all on a bacteria-covered Petri dish]*

(ii) Disc A – distilled water would not prevent growth of bacteria.
Disc B – low concentration of antibiotic, so there is a small clear zone where bacteria will not grow.
Disc C – higher concentration of antibiotic, so there is a larger clear zone where bacteria will not grow.
(iii) Disc A is a control, to show that it is the antibiotic which affects growth of bacteria.

## Question 5

(a) (i) A parasite is an organism which lives on or in another organism (the host). It causes the host harm.
(ii) A pathogen causes disease.
(b) Bacteria – growth is stopped or bacteria are killed.
Viruses – are not affected.
(c) (i) Passive – serum from previously infected animal.
Active – the body makes its own antibodies.
(ii) Passive immunity works more quickly.
(iii) If a person who has not already been vaccinated is exposed to a pathogen, e.g. is bitten by a rabid dog.
(iv) Live microbes would infect the person and cause disease.
Weakened/dead microbes will not cause disease, but they stimulate the body to make antibodies.
(d) (i) Plasmodium (a protozoan/protoctist)
(ii) It is carried by female mosquitoes (the mosquito acts as a vector).
When a mosquito bites a person, it sucks their blood. If the person is infected, Plasmodium will pass into the mosquito.
Plasmodium breeds inside the mosquito, to produce lots of offspring.
When the mosquito bites another person, it injects a small amount of saliva into the blood to stop it clotting.
The mosquito saliva contains Plasmodium, so this person gets infected.
Plasmodium reproduces asexually inside the human (in blood and in the liver) and causes cell damage and illness. This is malaria.
(iii) 1 Use insect repellent/mosquito nets to avoid being bitten.
2 Use insecticide to kill mosquitoes.
3 Drain ponds/swamps where mosquitoes breed to reduce mosquito numbers.

## part IV
# Timed practice paper with answers

# Timed practice paper

In this part of the book, we suggest you try to complete a whole exam paper in the time available to you in an examination. In GCSE Biology there is normally no choice of questions to be answered, but it is vital that you pace yourself properly during the exam.

### Before you begin
- Check that you have all the equipment you will need, e.g. pens, pencil, rubber, ruler, calculator, a watch or clock.
- Set an alarm clock for exactly 1 hour and 30 minutes.

### During the exam
- Check the number of questions you will have to answer as soon as you are told to start. Work out roughly how long you should spend on each question.
- Use the number of marks as a guide to how much you should write.
- Keep an eye on the time and regularly check your progress against the clock.
- Use any spare time to check your answers.

### When you are marking your answers
- Be strict with yourself. Give yourself the mark if you have written the key point of the answer – not just if that is what you meant to write.
- Make sure you have included important words or units in your answer to gain full marks.

> This practice paper is made up of questions from different examination boards, and should take 1 hour 30 minutes to complete

## TIMED PRACTICE PAPER

### Question 1
(a) The table below shows named human cells and plant cells. Complete the table to explain how each labelled part helps the cell with an important function. The first one has been done for you. [5]

| Name of cell | Diagram of cell | How the labelled part helps the cell |
|---|---|---|
| Red blood cell | Large area of cell membrane | Allows the cell to take in more oxygen |
| Sperm | Long tail | |
| Ovum (egg cell) | Large amount of cytoplasm | |

| Name of cell | Diagram of cell | How the labelled part helps the cell |
|---|---|---|
| Neurone (nerve cell) | Long nerve fibre | |
| Leaf (pallisade) cell | Many chloroplasts | |
| Root hair cell | Large area of cell membrane | |

(b) All the cells in the table, other than the red blood cell, have TWO parts in common. Name them. [2]

(c) Some human cells contain 46 chromosomes, some contain 23 chromosomes and some contain no chromosomes.
Complete the table below by writing in the number of chromosomes in each named human cell. You may use each number once, more than once or not at all. The first one has been done for you.

| Human cell | Number of chromosomes |
|---|---|
| Muscle cell | 46 |
| Sperm | |
| Ovum (egg cell) | |
| Neurone (nerve cell) | |
| Red blood cell | |

[4]
[ULEAC]

### Question 2
(a) What is the main job of the circulatory system? [1]
(b) The diagram below shows a section through a human heart.

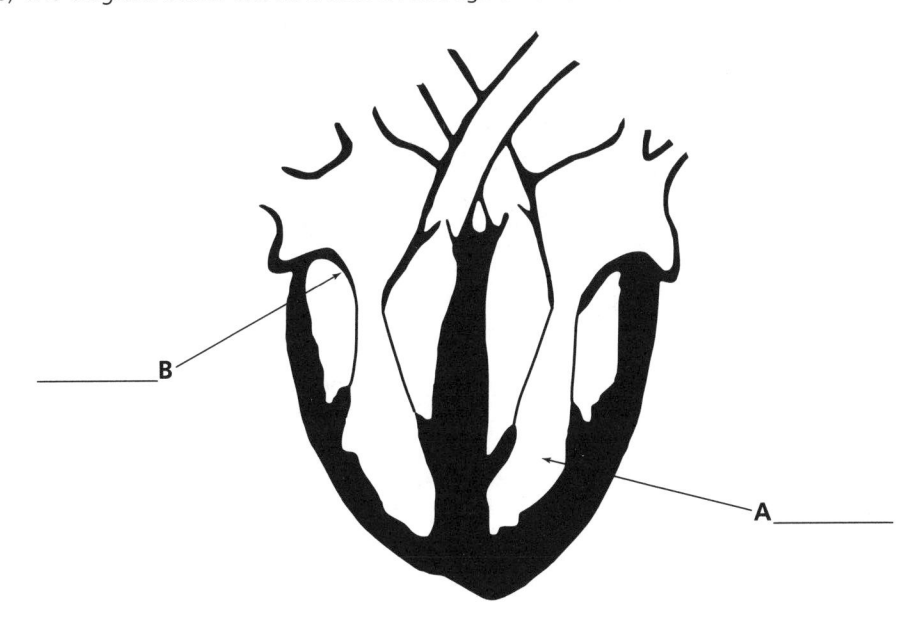

(i) Name the parts labelled A and B. [2]
(ii) On the diagram, draw arrows to indicate the direction of blood flow into, through and out of the left side of the heart. [3]
(iii) Explain, as fully as you can, how blood is forced to flow in this direction [2]

(c) The diagram below shows a white blood cell.

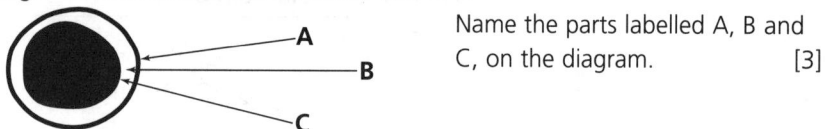

Name the parts labelled A, B and C, on the diagram. [3]

(d) (i) Give **two** ways in which white blood cells protect us from disease. [2]
(ii) Explain, as fully as you can, how immunisation protects us from disease. [3]

[NEAB]

## Question 3

The gene (allele) for blood clotting can mutate to a recessive form which can give rise to haemophilia, which is a sex linked disorder.

(a) Explain what is meant by a sex linked disorder. [2]
(b) The diagram is of the family tree of Queen Victoria, showing the inheritance of haemophilia.

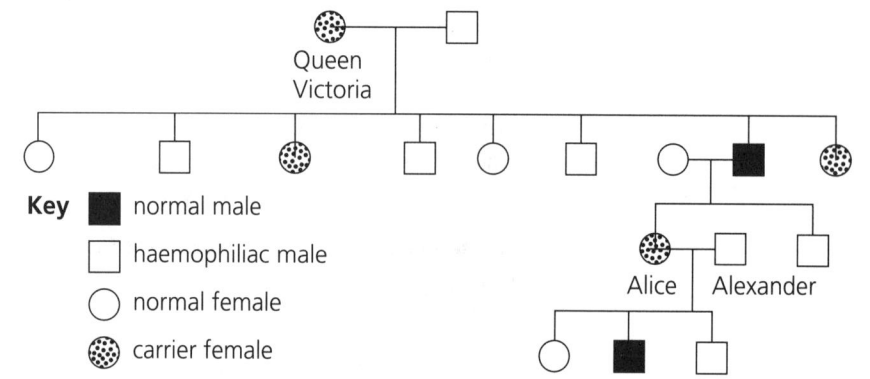

Key
■ normal male
□ haemophiliac male
○ normal female
⊛ carrier female

Use the symbols
$X^H$ = X chromosome with normal gene (allele)
$X^h$ = X chromosome with recessive gene (allele)
Y = Y chromosome
and the information in the family tree to explain how Alice and Alexander had one son who was a haemophiliac and one who was normal.
(A Punnett square must be used in your answer.) [4]

[NICCEA]

## Question 4

Scientists have found that a type of bacterium living in soil produces a protein which kills insects. Using genetic engineering, scientists have been able to develop tomato plants which can also make this protein.

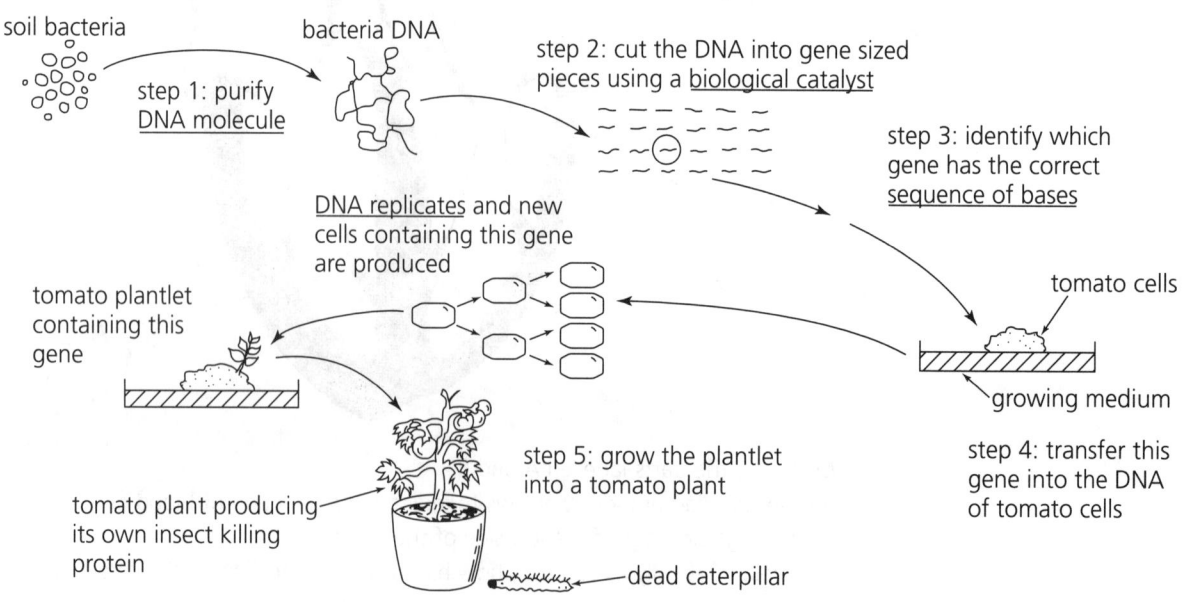

soil bacteria
step 1: purify DNA molecule
bacteria DNA
step 2: cut the DNA into gene sized pieces using a biological catalyst
step 3: identify which gene has the correct sequence of bases
DNA replicates and new cells containing this gene are produced
tomato cells
tomato plantlet containing this gene
growing medium
step 4: transfer this gene into the DNA of tomato cells
tomato plant producing its own insect killing protein
step 5: grow the plantlet into a tomato plant
dead caterpillar

(a) Explain what you understand by the four underlined phrases.
DNA molecule
biological catalyst
sequence of bases
DNA replicates [8]
(b) Suggest why some scientists are concerned about aspects of genetic engineering [4]

[MEG]

## Question 5

(a) The diagram below shows part of the carbon cycle which uses and replaces carbon dioxide in the air.

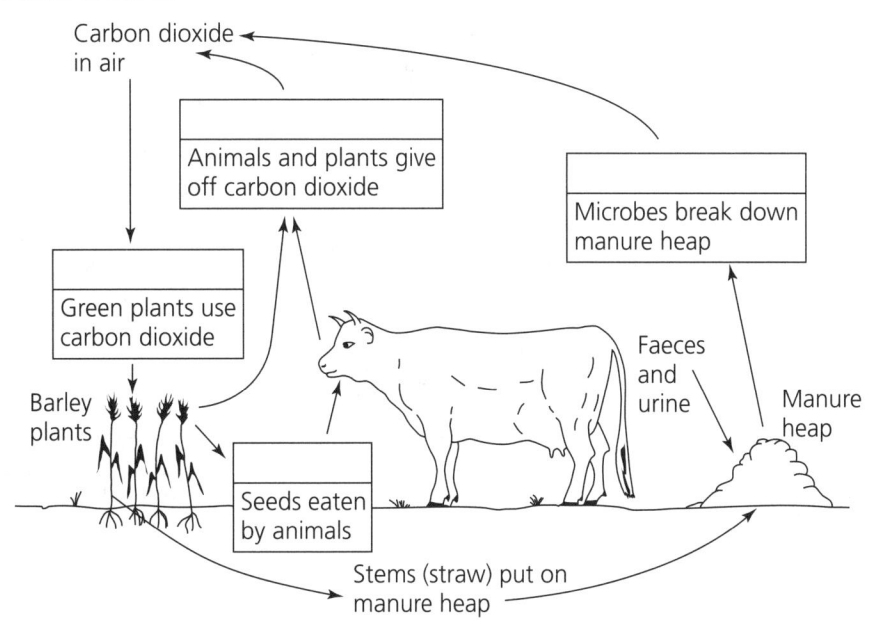

Use the diagram and your own knowledge to answer the following questions.

(i) These processes are part of the carbon cycle.

Decay
Excretion
Feeding
Photosynthesis
Respiration

Write the name of a process in each box in the diagram. Descriptions are given in each box to help you. [4]

(ii) Until 1993, farmers were allowed to burn straw after the harvest.
What effect did this have on the amount of carbon dioxide in the air? [1]

(iii) Some trees and some microbes growing millions of years ago did not decay completely after they had died. Use words from the list to complete the sentences below.

**burned    coal    fossil    gas    liquid    oil    sold    solid**

These trees became ................ and the microbes became ................
These are both ................ fuels and can be ................ to release energy. [4]

(b) The list below gives the names of three processes which are part of the nitrogen cycle.

Nitrogen fixation
Nitrification
Denitrification

Complete the table by writing in the name of the correct process in each box provided. Each process may be used once, more than once or not at all.

| Description of process | Name of process |
|---|---|
| Nitrate is changed into nitrogen gas | |
| Nitrogen gas is used by bacteria in root nodules of bean plants which help the plants make protein | |
| Faeces are broken down by microbes and used to make nitrates | |
| Nitrogen gas and oxygen are changed to nitrates by lightning | |

[4]

[ULEAC]

## Question 6
(a) The table lists the diets of several pond animals.

| Animal | Diet |
|---|---|
| Leech | phantom fly larva, pond snails |
| Mayfly larva | algae, dead plants |
| Flatworm | dead animals |
| Great diving beetle larva | phantom fly larva, mayfly larvae, flatworms, leeches |
| Pond snail | algae, dead plants |
| Waterflea | algae |
| Phantom fly larva | waterfleas |

(i) Use this information to complete the food web.

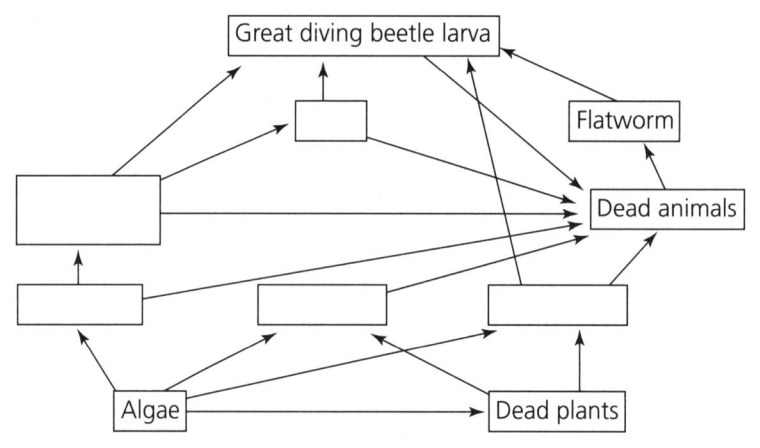

[5]

(ii) What is the original source of energy in the food web? [1]
(iii) Explain what the arrows in the food web show. [2]
(iv) Scavengers feed on either dead plant or animal remains. Name a scavenger in the pond food web. [1]

(b) The following data was collected by sampling a pond in Ireland.

| Type of organism | Number per 1000 m$^3$ |
|---|---|
| Producers | 300 |
| Primary consumer | 400 |
| Secondary consumer | 20 |
| Tertiary consumer | 1 |

(i) From the information in the table construct a pyramid of numbers on the grid provided. [3]

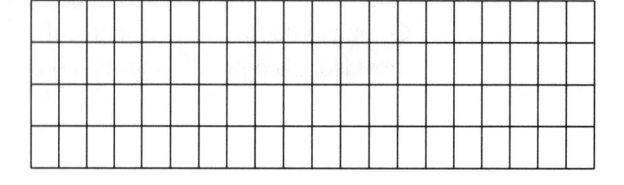

(ii) Draw a sketch of the pyramid of biomass you would expect to find in the lake. [2]
(c) The graphs shows the population of waterfleas and the algae they eat during the first six months of a year.

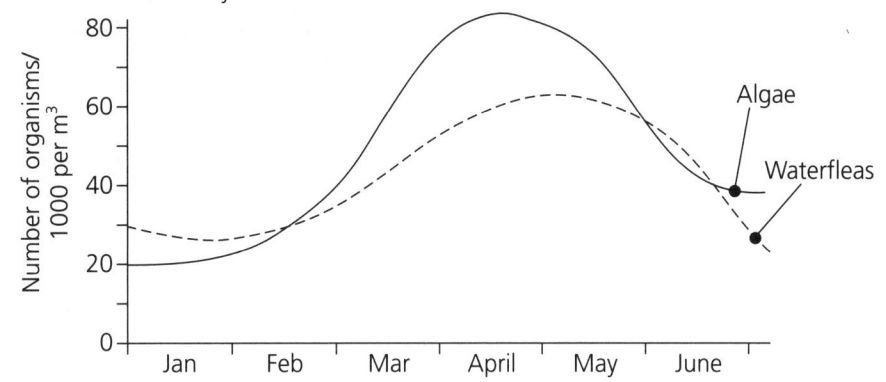

Use the information in the graph to help answer the following questions.
(i) Describe **one** similarity and **one** difference between the curves shown on the graph. [2]
(ii) Explain the changes in the population of algae between January and April. [2]
(iii) The size of the waterflea population can be calculated from the birth rate, death rate, immigration and emigration.
Explain how these act to cause the growth of a population. [3]

[NICCEA]

## Question 7

Organisms in a river may be affected by pollution. The statements in Table 1 below describe the effects on organisms of sewage flowing into a river. They are in the wrong order.

**Table 1**

| Statement | Letter |
|---|---|
| Algae near the surface of the river absorb nitrates and grow in large numbers | A |
| Bacteria break down the sewage into nitrates | B |
| Increased algae prevent light from reaching plants growing on the river bed | C |
| Plants on river bed die | D |
| Sewage flows into the river | E |

Complete Table 2 by writing a letter (A, B, C, D or E) in each empty box to show the correct order of events after sewage enters a river. The first one has been done for you.

**Table 2**

| Order of events | First | Second | Third | Fourth | Fifth |
|---|---|---|---|---|---|
| Letter | E | | | | |

[4]

# OUTLINE ANSWERS

## Question 1

(a)

| Name of cell | How the labelled part helps the cell |
|---|---|
| Sperm | Long tail allows the sperm to **swim** to the ovum to fertilise it |
| Ovum | Large amount of cytoplasm contains **stored food** to give the embryo energy to grow |
| Neurone | Nerve fibre carries **nerve impulses** from one cell to another |
| Palisade cell | Chloroplasts **trap light energy** for photosynthesis |
| Root hair cell | Allows the cell to absorb more **water/minerals** [5] |

(b) 1 nucleus  2 cell membrane  3 cytoplasm  (Any two of these gain 1 mark each)

(c)

| Human cell | Number of chromosomes |
|---|---|
| Muscle cell | 46 |
| Sperm | 23 [1] |
| Ovum (egg cell) | 23 [1] |
| Neurone (nerve cell) | 46 [1] |
| Red blood cell | 0 [1] |

**Remember:** Gametes are haploid: they have half the normal number of chromosomes. Red blood cells have no chromosomes at all. [4]

**Total = 11 marks**

## Question 2

(a) To move substances around the body [1].

(b) (i) A = left ventricle [1]   B = tricuspid valve [1]

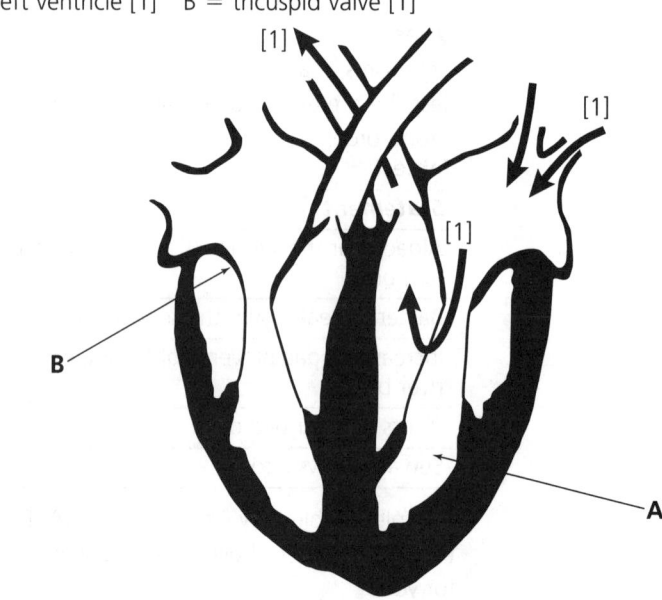

(ii) [diagram of heart with labels A and B, arrows marked [1]]

(iii) When the atrium contracts, pressure rises, so blood is forced into the ventricle [1].
When the ventricle contracts, pressure rises, so blood is forced into the artery [1].
Valves close to prevent backflow of blood [1].           (Maximum = 2 marks)

(c) A = cell membrane   B = cytoplasm   C = nucleus           [3]

(d) (i) 1  Some white blood cells (lymphocytes) make chemicals called antibodies. These stick to germs and destroy them [1].
    2  Some white blood cells (phagocytes) can change shape to surround and engulf germs. The germs are then destroyed [1].

(ii) A person is vaccinated with dead microbes (or a weakened strain) [1].
These do not cause disease, but they stimulate lymphocytes to make antibodies [1].
If the person is infected by that type of microbe in the future, the lymphocytes can 'remember' how to make antibodies [1].
Antibodies quickly kill the microbes, and prevent the person becoming ill [1].
           (Maximum = 3 marks)

**Total = 16 marks**

# timed practice paper with answers

## Question 3

(a) The faulty gene is carried on the X chromosome [1].
The disease is more common in men than women [1].

(b) Alice = carrier female = $X^H X^h$
Alexander = normal male = $X^H Y$      [1] for correct genotypes of parents

Parents     $X^H X^h$      $X^H Y$
Gametes    $X^H$   $X^h$     $X^H$   Y     [1] for correct gametes
F1

| | $X^H$ | Y |
|---|---|---|
| $X^H$ | $X^H X^H$ | $X^H Y$ |
| $X^h$ | $X^H X^h$ | $X^h Y$ |

[1] for Punnett square

$X^H X^H$ = normal female
$X^H Y$ = normal male
$X^H X^h$ = carrier female
$X^h Y$ = haemophiliac male

The normal son was $X^H Y$      [1] for correct genotypes of offspring
The haemophiliac son was $X^h Y$

**Total = 6 marks**

## Question 4

(a) There are two marks available for each explanation. Make sure you include two separate points in each case: any of the following would be worth one mark (maximum = eight).

**DNA molecule**
A large molecule which is a double helix shape.
Chromosomes are made of DNA, so it is the bacterial chromosome which is being purified.
This molecule carries genetic information/thousands of genes.

**Biological catalyst**
This is an enzyme.
It speeds up rates of reaction (here, breakdown of DNA).
It is biological because it is made inside living organisms.

**Sequence of bases**
DNA contains four types of bases.
These are Adenine, Thymine, Cytosine and Guanine.
The order of the bases makes up the genetic code.
Bases are read in groups of three (a triplet, or codon).
Each triplet codes for one amino acid.

**DNA replicates**
Replicates means makes an exact copy of itself.
This happens just before cell division, so that each new cell gets a complete set of genes.
The DNA double helix unwinds and bonds between the bases are broken.
Spare bases line up against the DNA strands by base pairing.
Adenine links with Thymine, Cytosine links with Guanine.
New pieces of DNA are formed.

(b) Avoid general statements like 'it is not natural' or 'it is interfering with nature'. Try to explain risks to humans, to other organisms, or to the environment. The following are some of the points you could make, but there are lots of others (maximum = four).
Genetically engineered bacteria could cause disease in humans or other organisms.
Genetically engineered plants could begin to grow wild and compete with native plants; native plants might decrease in numbers and become extinct.
Genetically engineered plants or animals could begin to grow wild and could upset the balance of natural food webs.
Genetically engineered animals may suffer as a result of the changes, e.g. cattle which grow faster may have painful joints and heart disease.
If we could genetically engineer humans, is it right to decide that some characteristics are better than others?

**Total = 12 marks**

## Question 5

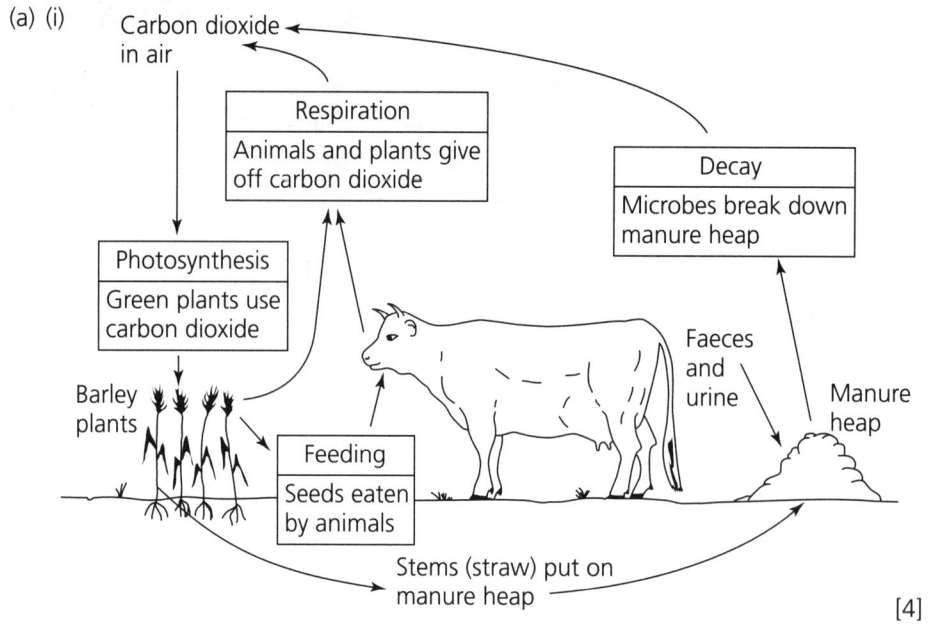

(a) (i) [Diagram showing carbon cycle with: Carbon dioxide in air; Respiration – Animals and plants give off carbon dioxide; Photosynthesis – Green plants use carbon dioxide; Decay – Microbes break down manure heap; Barley plants; Feeding – Seeds eaten by animals; Faeces and urine; Manure heap; Stems (straw) put on manure heap] [4]

(ii) Burning increases carbon dioxide [1].

(iii) These trees became **coal** and the microbes became **oil**. These are both **fossil** fuels and can be **burned** to release energy [4].

(b)

| Description of process | Name of process |
|---|---|
| Nitrate is changed into nitrogen gas | Denitrification [1] |
| Nitrogen gas is used by bacteria in root nodules of bean plants which help the plants make protein | Nitrogen fixation [1] |
| Faeces are broken down by microbes and used to make nitrates | Nitrification [1] |
| Nitrogen gas and oxygen are changed to nitrates by lightning | Nitrogen fixation [1] |

**Total = 13 marks**

## Question 6

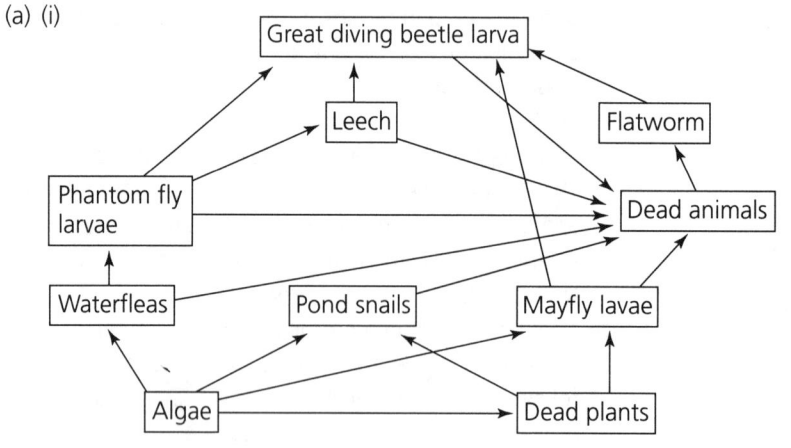

(a) (i) [Food web diagram showing: Great diving beetle larva, Leech, Flatworm, Phantom fly larvae, Dead animals, Waterfleas, Pond snails, Mayfly lavae, Algae, Dead plants]

[1 mark for each box completed correctly]

(ii) The Sun [1]

(iii) The arrows show how **energy** passes through the food web [1]. Energy is passed on when one organism eats another [1].

(iv) Flatworm/mayfly larva/pond snail [1].

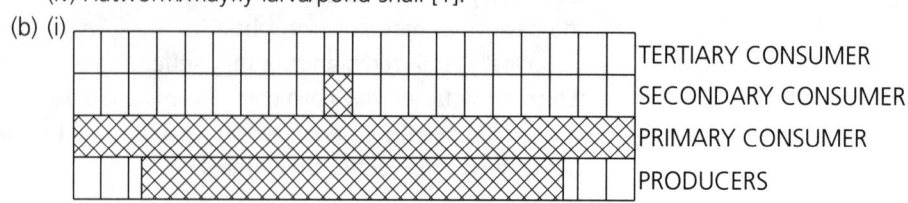

(b) (i) [Pyramid diagram with levels labelled: TERTIARY CONSUMER, SECONDARY CONSUMER, PRIMARY CONSUMER, PRODUCERS]

# timed practice paper with answers

The **pyramid of numbers** must be to scale on the grid provided.
One mark is for each trophic level drawn correctly [3].

(ii) The **pyramid of biomass** is a sketch: it should be this shape, but the exact width of the bars does not matter [2].

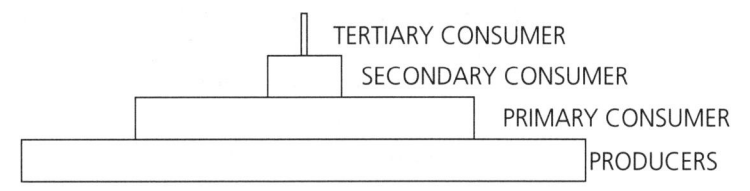

```
                    TERTIARY CONSUMER
                   SECONDARY CONSUMER
                    PRIMARY CONSUMER
                         PRODUCERS
```

(c) (i) **Similarity**:
Both populations are low in winter and higher in spring.
Both populations fall in summer.
The curves are the same shape.
**Difference**:
The number of algae rises before the number of waterfleas rises.
The number of algae falls before the number of waterfleas falls.
[Maximum: 2 marks; one similarity and one difference]

(ii) The number of algae rises between January and April [1] because there is more light available for photosynthesis [1] and because the temperature is warmer, so they can grow faster [1]. [Maximum = 2 marks]

(iii) Growth of a population occurs when:
birth rate is higher than usual [1];
death rate is lower than usual [1];
individuals join the population from other places (immigration) [1], and emigration is low (few individuals leave the population) [1]. [Maximum = 3 marks]

**Total = 21 marks**

## Question 7

| Order of events | First | Second | Third | Fourth | Fifth |
|---|---|---|---|---|---|
| Letter | E | B [1] | A [1] | C [1] | D [1] |

This is a description of eutrophication. Always read through all the statements before starting to write your answer, and check it again once you have finished.

**Total = 4 marks**

### Interpreting your mark

The total mark available for this practice examination paper was 83.
It is impossible to give the marks which are equivalent to a particular grade at GCSE because:
- the questions came from different examination boards;
- each examination board will set its own grade boundary marks, and these vary slightly from year to year;
- you would enter for a particular tier of paper (e.g. foundation or higher), and these questions are a mixture of both types.

*However, you can learn a lot from your score on this paper*
- To obtain a grade C at GCSE you should achieve 50–55% (that is equivalent to 42–46 marks on this paper).
- To obtain a grade A at GCSE you should achieve 65–70% (that is equivalent to 54–58 marks on this paper).
- You can tell which type of questions you find difficult, e.g.
  – short answer
  – completion/labelling of diagrams
  – sequencing of events

- extended prose answers, etc.

You can then practise more of this type of question.

▶ You can tell which areas of the syllabus you don't understand properly, or need to revise more thoroughly and can target your efforts on this.

▶ **If you are pleased with your mark**: well done, you are obviously on the right lines and you should carry on with your revision programme.

▶ **If you are disappointed with your mark**: don't give up! Look carefully at where you are losing marks and try some more past paper questions when you have done some more revision.

# LONGMAN EXAM PRACTICE KITS

## REVISION PLANNER

### Getting Started — *Begin on week 12*
Use a calendar to put dates onto your planner and write in the dates of your exams. Fill in your targets for each day. Be realistic when setting the targets, and try your best to stick to them. If you miss a revision period, remember to re-schedule it for another time.

### Get Familiar — *Weeks 12 and 11*
Identify the topics on your syllabuses. Get to know the format of the papers – time, number of questions, types of questions. Start reading through your class notes, coursework, etc.

### Get Serious — *Week 10*
Complete reading through your notes – you should now have an overview of the whole syllabus. Choose 12 topics to study in greater depth for each subject. Allocate two topic areas for each subject for each of the next 6 weeks

| No. of weeks before the exams | Date: Week commencing | MONDAY | TUESDAY |
|---|---|---|---|
| 12 | | | |
| 11 | | | |
| 10 | | | |

**LONGMAN EXAM PRACTICE KITS:**
Titles Available –

**GCSE**
Biology
Business Studies
Geography
Mathematics
Physics
Science

**A-LEVEL**
Biology
Business Studies
Chemistry
Mathematics
Psychology
Sociology

There are lots of ways to revise. It is important to find what works best for you. Here are some suggestions:

- try testing with a friend: testing each other can be fun!
- label or highlight sections of text and make a checklist of these items.
- learn to write summaries – these will be useful for revision later.
- try reading out loud to yourself.
- don't overdo it – the most effective continuous revision session is probably between forty and sixty minutes long.
- practise answering past exam papers and test yourself using the same amount of time as you will have on the actual day – this will help to make the exam itself less daunting.
- pace yourself, taking it step by step.

| WEDNESDAY | THURSDAY | FRIDAY | SATURDAY | SUNDAY |
|---|---|---|---|---|
|  |  |  |  |  |
|  |  |  |  |  |
|  |  |  |  |  |

LONGMAN

# LONGMAN EXAM PRACTICE KITS

## REVISION PLANNER

**LONGMAN EXAM PRACTICE KITS:**
Titles Available –

**GCSE**
- Biology
- Business Studies
- Geography
- Mathematics
- Physics
- Science

**A-LEVEL**
- Biology
- Business Studies
- Chemistry
- Mathematics
- Psychology
- Sociology

There are lots of ways to revise. It is important to find what works best for you. Here are some suggestions:

- try testing with a friend: testing each other can be fun!
- label or highlight sections of text and make a checklist of these items.
- learn to write summaries – these will be useful for revision later.
- try reading out loud to yourself.
- don't overdo it – the most effective continuous revision session is probably between forty and sixty minutes long.
- practise answering past exam papers and test yourself using the same amount of time as you will have on the actual day – this will help to make the exam itself less daunting.
- pace yourself, taking it step by step.

### Getting Started — *Begin on week 12*
Use a calendar to put dates onto your planner and write in the dates of your exams. Fill in your targets for each day. Be realistic when setting the targets, and try your best to stick to them. If you miss a revision period, remember to re-schedule it for another time.

### Get Familiar — *Weeks 12 and 11*
Identify the topics on your syllabuses. Get to know the format of the papers – time, number of questions, types of questions. Start reading through your class notes, coursework, etc.

### Get Serious — *Week 10*
Complete reading through your notes – you should now have an overview of the whole syllabus. Choose 12 topics to study in greater depth for each subject. Allocate two topic areas for each subject for each of the next 6 weeks

| No. of weeks before the exams | Date: Week commencing | MONDAY | TUESDAY | WEDNESDAY | THURSDAY | FRIDAY | SATURDAY | SUNDAY |
|---|---|---|---|---|---|---|---|---|
| 12 | | | | | | | | |
| 11 | | | | | | | | |
| 10 | | | | | | | | |

LONGMAN

# LONGMAN

## Get Revising — Weeks 9 to 4

Working on the basis of covering two topics per week an ideal pattern to follow for each week would be:

Read through your class notes and coursework.

Summarise the main points:
- write down the main principles/theories
- outline key terms and definitions
- note important examples/illustrations
- list important data/formula

(Using a highlighter pen is very useful here)

Practise answering exam questions:
- work through the questions in your Longman Exam Practice Kits
- write outline answers
- write full answers to some questions giving yourself the same time as in the exam
- make sure that you try to answer questions of each type set in the exam
- check your answers with those provided in your Longman Exam Practice Kit. Learn from any mistakes you have made.

## Get Confidence — Weeks 3 to 1

- Have a final read through of all your class notes and coursework.
- Read through the summaries you have already made.
- Try to reduce these summary notes to a single side of A4 paper.
- Test yourself to check that you can remember everything on each A4 page.
- Go over the practice questions already attempted.

### The day before the exams
- Read through each A4 summary sheet.
- Check that you have all the equipment you need for the exam.
- Do something you enjoy in the evening.
- Go to bed reasonably early: tired students rarely give their best.

### The exam – get up and go
- Have a good breakfast to give you energy.
- Don't panic – everyone else is nervous too.
- Remember – the examiners are looking for opportunities to give you marks, not take them away!

**Good luck!**

| No. of weeks before the exams | Date: Week commencing | MONDAY | TUESDAY | WEDNESDAY | THURSDAY | FRIDAY | SATURDAY | SUNDAY |
|---|---|---|---|---|---|---|---|---|
| 9 | | | | | | | | |
| 8 | | | | | | | | |
| 7 | | | | | | | | |
| 6 | | | | | | | | |
| 5 | | | | | | | | |
| 4 | | | | | | | | |
| 3 | | | | | | | | |
| 2 | | | | | | | | |
| 1 | | | | | | | | |